Friedrich Ebert 1871–1925

Walter Mühlhausen

Friedrich Ebert 1871–1925

A Social Democratic Statesman

Translated by Christine Brocks

DIETZ

Bibliografische Information der Deutschen Bibliothek

Die Deutsche Bibliothek verzeichnet
diese Publikation in der Deutschen Nationalbibliografie;
detaillierte bibliografische Daten sind im Internet
unter *http://dnb/ddb.de* abrufbar.

ISBN 978-3-8012-4228-2

Translated by Christine Brocks, Sheffield

Editorial support and photography-caption translation:
Sebastián Cuevas-Chapa / Collin Grismer

Cover design:
Jens Vogelsang, Aachen

Typesetting & layout:
Kempken DTP-Service | Satztechnik · Druckvorstufe · Mediengestaltung,
Marburg

Printing & production:
CPI – Ebner & Spiegel GmbH, Ulm

www.dietz-verlag.de

Contents

Appendix

Friedrich Ebert (1871–1925)

Prologue: A Social Democrat becomes Head of State

The date is 11 February, 1919. The place of events: Weimar, in Thuringia. The agenda of the National Assembly (*Nationalversammlung*), the first parliament of the republic, includes the presidential election. It is widely believed that Friedrich Ebert, chairman of the Social Democratic Party of Germany (SPD), will win the race and become the new head of state, the first president of the German Reich. After a mere thirty minutes the ballot count confirms what was expected by most. Ebert, who in this key moment of his campaign cuts the figure of an earnest and serious individual, becomes president with 277 out of 379 votes.

Thus, in the figure of Friedrich Ebert, a Social Democrat once vilified in the German Empire (*Kaiserreich*) as "enemy of the Empire" became Germany's first democratically elected head of state. This spelled out the new constitutional political order of the era: The successor to the Emperor was to be a representative of the socialist labour movement.

This was the pinnacle of the political career for the saddler journeyman from Heidelberg. The Social Democrat explained in his acceptance speech to the delegates what he understood his charge to be: "I intend to and will act as the representative of the whole German nation, and not as the leader of a single party." This commitment to non-partisanism became the leitmotif of the political career of the first *Reichspräsident*.

Still, Ebert remained strongly committed to his roots and the interests of the labour movement, declaring: "I nonetheless avow to being a son of the working class, brought up in the socialist tradition of thought, and shall never deny either my origins or my beliefs." Ebert stood until his death on 28 February 1925, at the age of 54, not only between the poles of state interests and party principles, but also at the head of a widely unpopular republic, one not only disliked by many, but also under constant foreign pressure.

I The Path of a Labour Leader (1871–1905)

1 Childhood, Youth, and Apprenticeship Years

His birthplace was a dwelling of about 50 square meters in the historical city centre of Heidelberg, where he was born into a family of tailors on 4 February 1871. Ebert was the seventh of nine children and spent his rather typical youth in a small craftsman's household. Just a few weeks before that the German Empire (*Kaiserreich*) had been summoned into existence in the French city of Versailles with the proclamation of King Wilhelm I of Prussia as Emperor of the German Empire. No one could have expected that a man with Friedrich Ebert's family background would become Germany's first democratic head of state a mere 48 years after Wilhelm I had been crowned German Emperor. When the Kaiserreich was proclaimed on 18 January 1871, the famous Social Democratic leader August Bebel was remanded into custody. Ebert would become the successor of that charismatic head of the Social Democratic Party in 1913.

Friedrich Ebert began his political career during his travels as a journeyman saddler. Not much is known about this period of his life since, as in the case of several other labour leaders with a family background similar to Ebert's, there are very few, if any, sources available from those days. Nothing is known about Ebert's education or about how his childhood and youth influenced his later life. In his family, there were nine children, three of which died in infancy or early-childhood. He and his family lived in a small, three-room flat in the narrow streets of Heidelberg's old town. This was the secure, although cramped, environment in which Ebert grew up. Even though his surroundings were proletarian, his family's home was almost petty bourgeois in character due to Ebert's father being one of the higher earners in his profession. In his youth, Ebert probably did not experience either dire need or poverty. However, it is very likely that living in a proletarian neighbourhood made him aware of social grievances.

From Easter 1877 until March 1885, Ebert attended primary school with average results. Upon leaving school, he began an apprenticeship as saddler. By the end of 1888, he started his journeyman years as planned, something common for craftsmen at that time. Although Ebert left home for good at the age of seventeen, he remained very much attached to Heidelberg for the rest of his life.

Ebert's political career and social development were closely linked to the rise of the Social Democratic Party in the Wilhelmine Kaiserreich. The young and still small workers' party wanted to achieve freedom, equality, and social justice. Ebert had already come into contact with Social Democratic ideas in his early childhood. However, it was his godfather Wilhelm Strötz, a well-known Social Democrat from Mannheim, who had a crucial impact on him and influenced his turn to the Social Democratic labour movement.

Consequently, the young saddler began his journey of two and a half years in near-by Mannheim, a stronghold of the socialist movement. After several stops in Southern Germany, he travelled north and stayed in Hanover for nearly a year, the longest time he spent in a city during his travels. His journeyman years coincided with the final stage of the Anti-Socialist Laws (1878–1890). At that time, Friedrich Ebert became a member of the saddlers' trade union and the Social Democratic Party. Wherever he stopped during his journey, he took part in building up union organisations and campaigned for the socialist cause. In this role, he felt the full impact of Chancellor Otto von Bismarck's policies aimed at taming the emerging labour movement – an attempt which ultimately failed. He witnessed first-hand how the German

Only four photographs remain of Friedrich Ebert from the time before his marriage at age 23: Here the young saddler at about 20 years of age.

society excluded Social Democrats as "men without a fatherland" (*vaterlandslose Gesellen*). He also experienced the power of solidarity within the labour movement during his time in Kassel, when he and his colleagues went on strike and ultimately achieved their political demands against their employer. After short stops in Brunswick, Wesel, Barmen, and Quakenbrück, Ebert travelled to Bremen, where he arrived in May 1891. This northern German city was one of the recent strongholds of the labour movement. Here, Ebert stayed for over fourteen years – fourteen years that were to shape him for the rest of his life.

2 From Party Activist to Party Functionary

The time in the Hanseatic city of Bremen was crucial for setting the course of Ebert's political and personal life. When he arrived in Bremen in 1891, he was a bachelor journeyman saddler and an ordinary, if diligent, party-soldier of the socialist labour movement with limited organisational skills. He was also a young agitator who had passed his baptism by fire as a public speaker, who had already gained experience in industrial strikes, and who had witnessed first-hand the solidarity of the socialist movement.

During his time in Bremen, Ebert acquired the political skills necessary for a party activist. By the time he left the Hanseatic city in 1905, he was well-known, even beyond regional borders, as a leading figure in the Social Democratic movement. Ebert then headed to Berlin, where he became a member of the executive committee of the SPD, henceforth playing a significant role in shaping the fate of the largest German political party. Initially, he had worked voluntarily and with great effort for the socialist movement. From 1900, however, he served the party as a professional politician and made a living off of politics, even though he additionally carried on with his work as a volunteer.

Ebert's time in Bremen also brought changes in his private life: In May 1894 he married the twenty-year old factory

Friedrich Ebert (right) with two friends in a studio 1894.

worker Louise Rump. She had been brought up in impoverished circumstances and was involved in the union movement. She was temporarily deputy chairwoman of a small union of woodworkers with only a few hundred members. Little is known about the marriage. Ebert's wife provided him with support; she always remained in the background and grew into the roles she was assigned due to her husband's political career, later gaining respect as the Reich president's wife. Five months after the wedding, their first child, Friedrich, was born. "A little revolutionary has arrived", read the birth announcement placed by his parents in the local Social Democratic newspaper, hinting at the fact that Social Democrats were considered revolutionaries in the Wilhelmine Kaiserreich. Three sons and one daughter followed: Georg (born in 1896), Heinrich (born in 1897), Karl (born in 1899), and Amalie (born in 1900). In 1917, Georg and Heinrich fell in combat during the First World War.

It was due to his tireless commitment, his skills as a public speaker, and his organisational abilities that Ebert had a successful career in the socialist movement. After only a short time, he became the "most zealous Social Democratic agitator", as a report by the Bremen police stated less than half a year after he had moved to the Hanseatic city. A tireless and sharp-tongued orator, Ebert was among the most-solicited speakers. He became a Social Democratic multi-functionary. He held several posts in the party and the socialist union movement during his time in Bremen. First, he was appointed chairman of the saddlers' association and, shortly afterwards, chairman of the union's executive committee. From 1894 to 1896, he was the leader of the local Social Democratic Party. At the same time, he held the post of Chairman of the Bremen Association of Publicans (*Verein der Bremer Wirte*). From 1897 onward, he headed the party's committee for agitation (*Landagitations-Komitee*) and was a member of several other socialist organisations. The plenitude of posts shows Ebert's tireless commitment to the socialist cause. At the same time, it illustrates the transition of the Social Democratic labour movement into a mass movement that required more and more voluntary functionaries. Thus, everything fell into place, and the tireless party-soldier Ebert found the increasingly differentiating political movement at a time when it needed senior leadership.

The young family in 1898: Friedrich Ebert with his wife and three sons (from left to right): Friedrich (born 1894), Georg (born 1896) and Heinrich (born 1897). Two more children would follow, Karl (born 1899) and Amalie (born 1900).

As a saddler, Ebert only slowly gained a foothold. His attempts to set up his own business failed. For some months in 1893, he worked as an editor at the "*Bremer Bürger-Zeitung*", the local Social Democratic newspaper. In 1894 he rented a pub. This was not a highly esteemed occupation with a generally high reputation. Among Social Democrats, however, publicans were regarded more positively due to the special role pubs played as places of sociability and agitation within the labour movement by the turn of the century. The pub was an integral part of proletarian counterculture. Ebert's pub ("*Bierhalle*") developed into a political meeting point for the labour movement in Bremen and a first port of call for workers seeking advice. The publican, who had autodidactically acquired extensive knowledge in social politics and social law, gave free legal advice to the workers; above all, in questions involving the constantly amended labour laws and social insurances. As long as Ebert was a publican, he did this voluntarily. Beginning in March 1900, he worked full-time as the first workers' secretary (*Arbeitersekretär*) in Bremen.

That was help on a small scale and rather unspectacular, but nonetheless important for the individual worker who found support in Ebert as an experienced advisor. The workers' secretaries were of significant importance in terms of their socio-political impact. As solicitor to the downtrodden, Ebert had to become acquainted with several socio-political areas, thus enriching his general legal knowledge. Also, the post as workers' secretary was one of the major career opportunities within the socialist labour movement. Due to Ebert's vast knowledge of several different legal areas, the "people's lawyer" was held in high esteem within his own ranks.

Ebert's professional reputation made him even more well-known. The majority of Social Democratic members of the German *Reichstag*, of the parliaments of the individual states, and the city councils, were recruited among the workers' secretaries. They also represented the SPD and the trade unions as designated experts in local committees. This was also true for Ebert, who was a member of the Bremen *Bürgerschaft* (state parliament of Bremen) from 1900 to 1905, where he led the Social Democratic faction.

As a social advisor to the working class, Ebert had to face all the hardships of the proletariat on a day-to-day basis. This work profoundly influenced the views he espoused in the ideological battles within his party between reformists, revisionists, and revolutionaries. Ebert detested theoretical debates and ideological disputes as not being helpful for practical work. Ebert never gave ideological and programmatic discussions the importance they enjoyed at the annual party congress. Convinced of the accuracy of the theoretical foundation as written in the fundamental party programme of Erfurt in 1891, Ebert regarded the practical everyday work as the Social Democratic Party's main task. In a speech he delivered in 1902, Ebert, the pragmatist, stated his desire to achieve democracy and social progress through reform: "We aim to abolish any kind of class-based society and demand the complete political equality of all without exception."

In the Bremen Bürgerschaft, however, he experienced how much painstakingly detailed work it took to wrest concessions from the unwieldy Wilhelmine system. Here, the chairman of the parliamentary group of the SPD appeared as an eloquent public speaker, who primarily addressed social issues and, in so doing, fell back on his fundamental knowledge as a workers' secretary. Even though Ebert's efforts in the Bürgerschaft bore little fruit, he carried on with his work there. The state parliament was the stage which presented the opportunity to advertise his political goals and call attention to social grievances from beyond his party. The Social Democratic initiatives revealed that the political system was indeed one, based on class rule. This again strengthened class consciousness and solidarity among Social Democratic followers.

Friedrich Ebert (centre) as one of the two presidents of the SPD Party Convention in September 1904 in Bremen.

Ebert's above-average commitment to the labour movement made the head of the local SPD in Bremen a political leader, well-known even beyond regional borders. He attracted the attention of the party leaders in Berlin for his adept organisational skills shown at the annual convention of the Social Democratic Party held in Bremen in 1904, which was, unlike previous congresses rife with fiery programmatic debates, not only relatively harmonious but also the highlight of Ebert's political career in the Hanseatic city. One year later, he was elected into the executive committee of the SPD.

Thus, his wish to leave the Hanseatic city came true. Theoretical and strategic disputes within the local party had crippled practical work in Bremen. Changes in personnel had weakened Ebert's reformist position within the local party organisation, which seemed to become ever more dominated by radical views. Being a reformist, this shift of power within the party sparked his desire for personal change. Although the different political groups in the party still agreed on basic Social Democratic principles, Ebert no longer felt politically comfortable in Bremen. As he wrote, he was "profoundly put off" primarily by the hostility dominating the discussions. He hoped that "a change of location would be best to escape the dilemma".

The problem was solved just a few months after he had written these lines. On 24 September 1905, the delegates of the SPD party congress in Jena, a city in Thuringia, elected Ebert as party secretary, a newly created full-time post within the executive committee of the party. The SPD-headquarters in Berlin was in need of an administrative expert. Ebert had demonstrated his competence in this field. He had built up the workers' secretariat in Bremen and successfully chaired it for five years. The person for the new post was supposed to work exclusively at the party offices without being burdened with other tasks, such as a parliamentary seat. All this applied to Ebert. Apparently, he had made a permanent impression as a skilful organiser and facilitator with both party leaders and delegates from all over Germany due to his handling of the party conference in Bremen.

When Ebert headed to Berlin in December 1905, he had already become a nationally well-known leader with the experience of a multi-tasking functionary. He had learned Social Democratic party work from scratch and made his way up from a volunteer position to a professional post thanks to his tireless commitment. However, he had also witnessed that disputes over the political direction of the party hampered practical work, and that there was a tendency among Social Democrats to tear each other apart over programmatic issues. Politically, his grass-roots work as a publican, who was often asked for advice, and as a workers' secretary had profoundly influenced him. Someone who, like Ebert, closely faced all the worries and hardships of the workers developed a special sense for both the necessity of social progress and the politically attainable. He championed improvements which would inure to the benefit of the working class there and now and thought little of feeding the workers' hopes of a utopian society in the distant future. Even though Ebert basically accepted the party's programmatic Marxist foundations, he was above all a pragmatist adverse to theory, in contrast to the revolutionary rhetoric of Social Democracy. This did not change during the years when Ebert was a member of the executive of the Social Democratic Party.

II Leader of the Social Democratic Party (1905–1918)

1 Organiser of the Mass Party

Friedrich Ebert was one of the first representatives of a second generation of leaders at the party executive committee. He and Hermann Müller, who would be elected as a party leader one year after Ebert, were the youngest members of the executive, located in the Lindenstraße in Berlin, where they worked together with the chairmen and founding fathers of the labour movement August Bebel and Paul Singer. Ebert's years on the party executive committee were characterised by the needs of the rapidly growing SPD, which increased from about 380,000 members in 1905-6 to more than a million in 1914. Ebert's predominant task was to contribute to the reorganisation of the party structure in order to make it altogether more effective. Accordingly, his functions were primarily organisational and administrative. In his everyday work, he had to take care of tiring and detailed work, which nevertheless was essential for the functioning of the party as an organisation. Ebert made sure that those organisations and party newspapers all over the country, which had run into financial difficulties, got the support they needed, that advertising material was ordered, and that agitation tours and nationwide protest meetings were organised. In many cases, the party executive committee in Berlin made decisions about the staffing of editors of the numerous party newspapers.

Even outside of his own party, Ebert gained a reputation as a bureaucrat after a short period of time, a notion which was often used contemptuously against him. It did not reflect the manifold tasks he was entrusted with. For instance, from 1907 onwards, party relations with the socialist Free Trade

Unions fell under his responsibility. He was the liaison between the party executive committee and the trade union general commission. In addition to that, he became chairman of the "Central Office for the Working Youth of Germany" (*Zentralstelle für die arbeitende Jugend Deutschlands*) founded by the SPD and trade unions in 1908. As a vanguard organisation, it fit into the Social Democratic counterculture to the bourgeois society. The youth organisation was one part of the comprehensive social network which ideally would accompany every Social Democrat "from the cradle to the grave".

Soon Ebert became increasingly involved in the programmatic disputes and philosophical skirmishes that shook the mass party. In 1908, at the party convention in Nuremberg, Ebert delivered the closing words on behalf of the party executive on the controversial issue of the parliamentary approval of the budget in place of the ill chairman, August Bebel. Social Democratic parliamentary groups of some southern German diets had voted in favour of the state budgets. In so doing, they had violated the official party line – "not a penny and not a man for this system". At the Nuremberg party convention in 1908, Ebert made the parliamentary approval of the budget a question of principle for the party and demanded recognition of previous resolutions. Political actions were to be based on a united front presented by the party as a whole. Ebert proclaimed:

> "The unity of the party is the precondition for our success. This, however, requires that the minority bows to the majority, that every single member respects and recognises the convention's resolutions. If that no longer happens […] it will cripple the party's political efficacy and its clout."

In ideological debates on socialist theory and on the mass strike as a political weapon, Ebert always took the view of

Group photograph with a woman: the SPD-executive committee at the party congress in Leipzig in September 1909; Back row: (from left to right) Luise Zietz, Friedrich Ebert, Hermann Müller, and Robert Wengels; front row: (from left to right) Alwin Gerisch, Paul Singer, August Bebel, Wilhelm Pfannkuch, Hermann Molkenbuhr.

the party executive. He did so at several regional party conventions and meetings, where he appeared as a speaker on behalf of the party executive and urged the recognition of the party resolutions. Ebert, a representative of the political centre of the party, aimed at reconciliation between the diverging party wings. He made a mark as mediator and moderator in programmatic and ideological disputes which had almost brought the party to the brink of splitting in the pre-war period. One of his crucial tasks was to defuse conflicts in regional organisations. It was, however, inevitable that his work was not always appreciated among members of a party shaken by debates about its future course.

In addition, his efforts were not always successful. In Württemberg, for instance, positions between moderate reformists and radical revolutionaries in the state party organisation had hardened and almost split up the SPD. When Ebert tried to mediate there on behalf of the party leadership, he drew the ire of both sides. Many reformists from southern Germany regarded him as the actual stirrer among the members of the party executive in the far away capital.

Where did Ebert stand in the wide political range of the pre-war Social Democratic Party, from radical revolutionaries to pragmatic reformists? He was one of the pragmatists and leaned towards the party manifesto. He detested nothing more than the theoretical debates still smouldering within the labour movement. In his view, these debates only distracted from the actual crucial political tasks and jeopardised the clout of the party. Ebert is best classified as a representative of the political centre of his party. For him, the unity of the Social Democratic movement was the greater good and the foundation of political power necessary to reform, and finally, overcome the existing system. Already during his time in Bremen, he had condemned the disputes at the annual party conventions, which sometimes became personal. The debate of the revisionists' argument for the party platform rekindled after the SPD party convention in Dresden in 1903. They intended to convert the revolutionary manifesto into a reformist party program. Ebert highly disapproved of these debilitating disputes: "In the future, when we have to do our washing, we should go into the washhouse instead of airing our dirty linen in public." In his eyes, internal conflicts were acceptable as long as the party appeared united in public. That was his guideline.

Ebert developed into one of the most important functionaries of the party executive. He was an adroit tactician in party and administrative matters. Also, he stood out as a public speaker, organiser, and agitator with a high level of energy, efficiency, and experience. Whilst Ebert was by no means uncontroversial as a party functionary during his time in Bremen, he became one of the leading figures of German Social Democracy and the "man of action" in the headquarters after he had joined the party executive as secretary. Compared to his colleagues of the executive, Ebert undoubtedly had the most experience in practical political work. He was sent to regional organisations as the executive's emissary, where he acted as keeper of party resolutions and mediator of disputes. Ebert organised the internal operations of the party office and coordinated nationwide party campaigns such as election campaigns and suffrage demonstrations. All this explains why he was nominated to replace the deceased party leader Paul Singer at the party convention in Jena in 1911. Although Ebert explicitly declined the candidacy, he received 102 votes. Hugo Haase, who was favoured by the party leadership, was elected with 283 votes. By not running for the post, Ebert had complied with the party leadership in order to avoid impending debates on direction, which would have had damaging effects on the party's results in the Reichstag elections in January 1912. His compliance was essential to demonstrate party unity. There was probably another reason why Ebert rejected the highest post in the party when it had been within his grasp: he still did not have a seat in the Reichstag. He would achieve this just a few months later.

Ebert had failed to win a seat in the Reichstag three times: in 1898, in 1903, and in 1906. Finally, in 1912, he was successful in the constituency in Elberfeld-Barmen (today's Wuppertal). Although Ebert missed the required overall majority in the first round by just a few votes, he subsequently won in the second round against the previous Member of Parliament, a Free Conservative. After these last pre-war Reichstag elections, the Social Democratic Party had a majority of 110 seats out of a total of 397 and was the largest party in the German Reichstag. Ebert rarely addressed parliament in the time before the First World War, even if one of the great issues of the day was discussed. Unlike Philipp Scheidemann, his co-member of the party executive since 1911, Ebert did not make his career via parliament but within the party organisation.

The fact that Ebert was supposed to succeed the "workers' emperor" (*Arbeiterkaiser*) August Bebel after his death shows the high degree of universal appreciation for his political work at the SPD headquarters. At the party convention in Jena on 20 September 1913, Ebert was elected as one of the party leaders together with Hugo Haase, winning 433 out of the 473 votes cast. That was his reward for more than twenty years of tireless work for the party. He had earned the trust of the members and of the majority of the functionaries, although he did not have the confidence of the party's radical left due to his reformist views. Nevertheless, he was deemed capable of holding the SPD together in spite of the diverging ideas and wings developing within it.

Ebert was neither willing nor able to be a new Bebel. As a mass party, the SPD did not need a charismatic leader but a pragmatic organiser and, above all, a collective leadership. Ebert was precisely the right man for such a task. He was a representative of the political centre of the party, and he focused on the politically feasible. Neither did he want to get involved in visionary politics nor did he dream of the "great crash" or the sudden breakdown of the existing system. His political view was instead shaped by his belief in change through progress. In this, the new leader was representative of the party majority, though it still appeared to be dominated by radicals and their revolutionary slogans. Despite being verbally radical, the SPD on the eve of the First World War was not a revolutionary but a reformist party whose members believed in the power of the ballot and sought after improvements, political democracy, and social reform by legal means.

Friedrich Ebert had made his way in a legally operating party that had moved unstoppably from one election victory to another. This development had shaped Ebert's belief in gradual change. As party functionary and Hugo Haase's co-chairman, it was important for him to give more clout to Social Democracy in order to wrest reforms from the imperial bourgeois state. However, his time as party leader was overshadowed by the First World War which would shake the world and German Social Democracy to the core a year later.

2 Party Leader during the First World War

On 4 August 1914, a few days after the outbreak of the war, the Social Democratic parliamentary group in the Reichstag approved the war spending bill. This came as a surprise to the public, since in doing so the party contradicted its own iron principle of conceding to the system neither a penny nor a man. By approving the war credits, the Social Democrats, who had declared war against the system, supported the imperial war effort and sealed the *Burgfrieden* (civic truce) policy. With this cross-party truce, they refrained from their former fundamental opposition to the imperial regime. Right from the beginning, Ebert was a strong advocate of the Burgfrieden policy.

The international crisis following the assassination of the heir to the Austro-Hungarian throne in Sarajevo took the Social Democratic Party by surprise. At that time, Friedrich Ebert was on holiday on the Baltic island of Rügen with his wife and two of his children. On 28 July 1914, he interrupted his holidays due to the imminent danger of war and went back to Berlin. The Social Democratic leadership decided to send Ebert and Otto Braun, the party treasurer, to Switzerland in order to secure party funds and to be able to organise the party from abroad in case of potential repressions by

Holidays on the island of Rügen in the Baltic Sea in July 1914: Ebert interrupted his vacation and returned to Berlin on 28 July, due to the deteriorating international situation resulting from the assassination of Franz Ferdinand, heir to the Austro-Hungarian throne, on 28 June in Sarajevo, which would lead to the First World War.

the regime. However, the German government did not take action against the Social Democratic Party. Ebert returned on 4 August, right in time for the parliamentary vote on the spending bill. He wrote in his diary on 4 August 1914:

> "Berlin, 2 pm. I am on my way to the Reichstag. Scheidemann quickly briefs me about the meeting of the parliamentary group the day before. It is said to have been a tumultuous meeting, more tumultuous than ever before. Finally the group decided in favour of the war credits by 14 votes. I told Scheidemann that I would have voted as the majority had."

In fact, Ebert and his colleague in the party executive, Philipp Scheidemann, both sided with the majority in the SPD, expressing support for the war spending bill. During the first days of the war, Ebert and most of the Social Democrats firmly believed that Russia was the main aggressor against which Germany had to defend itself. The Tsarist regime had been the epitome of reaction and repression in the eyes of many Social Democrats long before the war. The SPD's belief that Russia was the aggressor was sincere, but mistaken, since Germany was responsible for the outbreak of the war to a high degree. Cunningly, the German government was successful in portraying the Tsar as the actual warmonger. The fear of despotic Tsarist rule confirmed the view held by Ebert and the majority of Social Democrats that Germany was forced to defend its national independence. In so doing, Ebert believed to be in accordance with the long-standing political commitment of the Social Democratic Party to national defence. The Social Democrats had always been committed to national defence, especially if Tsarist Russia, the symbol of reactionary oppression, were to be recognised as the putative war enemy. The former party chairman August Bebel, who had died in 1913, had left no doubt in 1904, when he proclaimed in the Reichstag that in the event of a war of aggression, the Social Democrats would "pick up their rifle and defend our German soil, to the very last man".

The national defence against a belligerent Russia was Ebert's key motive for his approval of the war credits on 4 August. Also, Ebert hoped that the government would reward the concessions being made and implement the parliamentarisation of the state and the democratisation of society long-desired by the Social Democratic Party. Nevertheless, the approval of the war credits was not a pledge meant to be converted into substantial reforms. Even in the spring of 1916, Ebert stressed in parliament that the Social Democratic Party would not demand a *quid pro quo* for its decision concerning the issue of national defence. That question should not become an "object of political haggling". After a while, however, he primarily demanded the abolition of the Prussian three-class voting system, which blatantly disadvantaged the workers. Social Democrats had been fighting and demonstrating against this form of franchise without success since the beginning of the century. Ebert defined "equal rights for all citizens in all areas" as a political goal from the beginning of the war. Nevertheless, he and the Social Democratic majority did not make their commitment to national defence conditional to the reaction of the government, or to any kind of political concession. National defence remained valuable in itself. The decision of 4 August led to a partial integration of Social Democracy into the state. Approving the war credits indicated the party's identification with the fate of the Reich. The Burgfrieden was not a watershed event, but rather a landmark on the way to the ultimate goal of integrating the SPD in the nation and reforming the state towards democracy. However, not all members of the SPD agreed with the Burgfrieden policy.

In general, both the party and the majority of the German population expected a short and victorious war. The party leadership intended to postpone all controversial issues until the early end to the fighting. It was, however, impossible in the long term to keep up the balancing act between the advocates and the opponents of the war credits, because the expectation of a quick victory proved to be illusory. Soon, the fighting developed into devastating trench warfare. The longer the war lasted, the more the individual groups in the SPD would express their political views.

The Burgfrieden policy finally led to a severe party crisis with which the SPD could not cope. Ebert tried to maintain the unity of the party, or "Bebel's legacy", as the Social Democratic leader called it. Unity was the guideline. That applied first and foremost during times of crisis, such as during the First World War, when Ebert virtually declared unity the party's imperative. His appeal to the party to maintain unity, however, was only successful in the short term given the burdens of the war and the severity of the decision.

The Burgfrieden policy within the Social Democratic Party crashed in December 1914, when the second war credits had to be approved. Karl Liebknecht, son of the party founder Wilhelm Liebknecht and representative of the left party wing, voted against the war spending bill. Liebknecht's stand against the second war credits bill in December 1914 made him the standard bearer of the war opposition. For the sake of party unity, Ebert withstood the pressure of the Social Democratic right wing for a long time. They wanted to edge out the opponents of the Burgfrieden policy as an annoying ballast as soon as possible. Ebert advocated the principle of party unity in public despite diverging views among party members. The vote of the parliamentary group had to be unanimous. Those who did not want to vote in line with the majority were allowed to abstain from the vote. The parliamentary group agreed on this procedure in February 1915. For Ebert, the minority must bow to the decision of the majority, otherwise the "organisational structure of the party", as he put it in November 1915, would dissolve. This was exactly what happened.

In December 1915, twenty oppositional Social Democrats voted against the war credits in the Reichstag. In Ebert's eyes, this was an inexcusable breach of party discipline. For him, the minority had destroyed the common political basis. His co-chairman Hugo Haase, who belonged to the oppositional minority, resigned as chairman of the parliamentary group. Ebert was elected as one of the three chairmen of the parliamentary group in his place.

Subsequently, the division between the opponents grew deeper. The continuously growing opposition in the party finally founded its own parliamentary group and, in April 1917, its own party, known as the Independent Social Democratic Party of Germany (*Unabhängige Sozialdemokratische Partei Deutschlands*; USPD) with Hugo Haase as its party leader. The result was a permanent split of Social Democracy

Deceptively idyllic family portrait from September 1916 during Heinrich's furlough (Heinrich would become a casualty of the war half a year later); (left to right) Friedrich Ebert, Amalie, Heinrich, Louise, Friedrich Jr., Karl. The son not photographed, Georg, would fall on the Western Front in May 1917.

from then on. This "battle of brothers", as Ebert accurately described the sharp confrontations between both Social Democratic parties in April 1917, drained the energy of the labour movement. Ebert was directly affected by this struggle, since the local party organisation of his constituency in Elberfeld-Barmen was sympathetic to the opposition regarding the war credits and finally joined the USPD.

During the First World War, the party found itself in the worst crisis since its founding days. Ebert had to face strains no other party leader had had to deal with since the end of the Anti-Socialist Laws in 1890, either to the same extent or over such a long period of time. Added to this were Ebert's personal worries about his sons Friedrich, Georg, and Heinrich, who had been conscripted. Friedrich, the eldest, was seriously injured in July 1916 and, after a long period of convalescence, had to rejoin the troops at the front in early 1917. Heinrich died in February 1917, and Georg was killed less than three months later. "We must console ourselves with the countless others who have lost their most beloved", wrote Ebert after Heinrich's death. The Ebert family had indeed experienced the same sorrow as millions of others who had lost loved ones.

It is safe to assume that these personal twists of fate had an impact on Ebert's politics even though there are no sources to prove this connection. The physical and emotional strain due to his workload during wartime is easily comprehensible. There was one conference after another. Countless meetings on party issues and with government representatives increased the stress on Ebert and his colleagues, even leading to physical or emotional breakdown. It is hard to say in which way these exertions and the deaths of his two sons affected Ebert's political actions. At the beginning of July 1917, however, Ebert complained impatiently about the inactivity of the government regarding democratic reforms at the "main committee" (*Hauptausschuss*), the most important parliamentary board between the Reichstag sessions:

> "Why all the grievous sacrifices, if the government is not inclined to grant us the most necessary, the most essential, the most natural in life, which is political equality, or if it is not prepared to abolish the fetters of political inequality, the three-class voting system?"

The reform of the Prussian suffrage laws, the abolition of the undemocratic three-class voting system, had become the cardinal question of domestic politics for Ebert. In the middle of 1917, it was, according to Ebert, high time for this reform. He did not accept any attempts of being put off until after the war. He asserted: "Mere promises are not enough." As early as April 1916, he had predicted that as soon as the soldiers would leave the trenches and return home they would not accept "being pushed in the political wire entanglements of the three-class voting system," but nothing happened. In March 1918, Ebert complained rightly, "the government did nothing the way it had agreed to. The government has duped us!" The leaders of the Reich remained passive. Nevertheless, it seemed that there was cooperation with the bourgeois parties in the offing.

In July 1917 the "Interparty Committee" (*Interfraktioneller Ausschuss*) with members of the SPD, the Catholic Centre Party, and the left-liberal Progress Party came into being. After years of exclusion, the SPD became a partner of the bourgeois parties. For the first time, Social Democrats were no longer politically isolated, and social boundaries had fallen away. The new majority for reform corresponded with the later Weimar Coalition, which would be the first republican government from February 1919 onwards. The first visible action of the Interparty Committee was the peace resolution, which passed the Reichstag on 19 July 1917. This resolution with the wording "peace of understanding" (*Verständigungsfrieden*) was largely in accordance with Social Democratic vocabulary and was opposed to the "victorious peace" (*Siegfrieden*) that the conservatives demanded in order to ultimately establish Germany as a world power through territorial annexations and economic hegemony. The Reichstag resolution, however, had little impact. Although the Interparty Committee was not very successful in the beginning, Ebert adhered to this first cross-party cooperation between the Social Democrats and the bourgeois parties at a national level. In his eyes, it was a significant step for the SPD on its way to becoming the governing party. Overall, the position of Social Democracy and that of Social Democrats gradually changed within the government structure. Having been excluded from power until 1914, the war brought the Social Democrats in ever increasing contact with the government, public agencies, and officials, especially in the numerous committees in the Reichstag.

Ebert's demands for political progress were answered before the war had been lost, and the Kaiserreich was ultimately forced to concede reforms. Whilst military defeat loomed and in spite of resistance from his own ranks, Ebert led his party to the first legitimate parliamentary government under the new Chancellor Max von Baden in the beginning of October 1918. It was, according to Ebert, the Social Democrats' "damned duty to step into the breach" in order to achieve the long-desired peace, to avoid a revolution, and to democratise the monarchy after the Emperor's abdication.

Ebert maintained his opinion, when the military leaders had to admit defeat on 2 October 1918, which until then had been thought impossible. Ebert, too, seemed to be broken. He could hardly hide his tears when he informed his parliamentary group about the state of affairs immediately after the military leaders had notified the party representatives of the dire situation. In view of the new circumstances, more and more Social Democrats in the Reichstag turned against participating in government. Otto Wels conjured his party friend Ebert: "Have you taken leave of your senses, just let those, who have carried on the war and are responsible for it and who have asked for the ceasefire, sign the peace treaty." Ebert had by no means "taken leave of his senses". According to his sober-minded assessment, he came to the conclusion that it was necessary to step into the breach in order to finish the war on acceptable terms and to take the chance to join the government. He showed decisiveness and finally won the support of the parliamentary group.

Thus, representatives of the SPD – Philipp Scheidemann and Gustav Bauer – became members of the first parliamentary government led by Chancellor Max von Baden. Ebert was not one of them, but he kept the party in line. By autumn 1918, Ebert's party as well as other governing circles recognized that the SPD-chairman had become one of the decisive personalities for further development of Germany. At the end of October 1918, a constitutional reform was approved which strengthened the position of the Reichstag against the government and ultimately converted the constitutional monarchy into a parliamentary system. For Ebert, this was the first crucial step towards the democracy he intended to achieve through political evolution instead of revolutionary disruption. Initially, he even wanted to maintain the monarchy, on condition that it would be converted, through further reforms, into a fully democratic system with the Emperor as head of state, playing merely a representative role. The Wilhelmine semi-parliamentary system should be transformed into a fully developed parliamentary government. This goal could even be accomplished under a monarchic head of state and did not necessarily imply a republic. However, the stubborn attitude of the government led Ebert to the conclusion that it was impossible to reform the German monarchy as an institution.

Yet constitutional reform came too late. The revolutionary movement, which had started in the harbour towns on the shores of the North and the Baltic Seas and was carried out by the war-weary masses, washed away Ebert's hopes on gradual transition. In the crucial days of autumn 1918, Ebert revealed his identification with the fate of the Reich, which he paired with an ethics of responsibility for his own and other parties. These were the key aspects that shaped his politics after the upheaval on 9 November 1918.

III People's Deputy during the Revolution (1918/19)

1 A Revolutionary against his Will

9 November 1918, shortly after 12 o'clock. Chancellor Prince Max von Baden received a delegation of the SPD in the Reich chancellery headed by the two party chairmen, Friedrich Ebert and Philipp Scheidemann. Due to the desperate military situation and the looming revolutionary crisis, the chancellor had just arbitrarily announced the abdication of Emperor Wilhelm II, thus fulfilling one of the key demands of the Social Democratic Party. Nevertheless, Friedrich Ebert insisted on transferring government power to those who have the "trust of the people" in order to prevent the revolution from turning into chaos and bloodshed. He demanded the appointment of a Social Democrat as chancellor. After brief consultation, Prince Max conceded the office of chancellor over to Ebert. The Social Democratic leader accepted, saying: "It is a difficult post, but I will do it."

In constitutional terms this was a highly questionable, albeit politically inevitable, course of action. It nevertheless marked a historical turn. The head of government of Imperial Germany had placed the fate of the dissolving Reich in the hands of the leader of the Social Democrats, a party that had been actively fought against and had been excluded from society since its very foundation in the 1860's. Still, the Prince of Baden was convinced that the pragmatic Social Democrat Friedrich Ebert would not pursue a radical path. By taking over the chancellorship, he would also oversee the liquidation of the Kaiserreich.

Although taken aback by the sudden breakdown of the German Empire, Ebert stepped into the breach. The key goals of the SPD were thus achieved: the Reich was parliamentarised, the completely discredited Emperor Wilhelm II had abdicated, and the SPD had become the governing party. In reflection of that, Ebert stated shortly after becoming chancellor, "Germany has completed its revolution." The course was set. He did not take any further steps towards the development of a political or institutional structure. Until 9 November, he could have agreed to a "monarchy with social character under a parliamentary system" – although not with Wilhelm II. The following events would, however, change everything.

In view of the revolution, which was rapidly spreading throughout the whole country, a highly visible sign was necessary to indicate a change of system, and this was the complete renunciation of the throne by the Hohenzollern and the German federal princes. They had to give up their crowns. Philipp Scheidemann, Ebert's party co-chairman since 1917, was much more aware of this than his colleague. By 2:00 pm on 9 November 1918, Scheidemann proclaimed the German Republic from the balcony of the Reichstag building. In so doing, he – according to Max von Baden – dealt a "final blow to the monarchy". Ebert criticised Scheidemann for declaring Germany a republic before the constitutional assembly had been convened: "You have no right to proclaim the republic. Only a constituent assembly can decide Germany's future – whether it will be a republic or something else."

Although Friedrich Ebert held the post as chancellor for only one day, he shaped politics in the subsequent period until the National Assembly met in February 1919. Ebert and the Majority Social Democrats had not wanted the revolution. Nevertheless, they were prepared to lead the movement in order to avoid chaos and anarchy. By 9 November, it was essential to act fast and fill the constitutional vacuum. Ebert showed a firm instinct for leadership and took the initiative. He urged the heads of the Reich authorities to remain in office and invited the Independent Social Democrats to join

"The new socialist chancellor" – Friedrich Ebert is the undisputed leader of the revolutionary government.

a coalition government. Initially, Ebert had favoured a broad government which would include the bourgeois centre parties. This was no longer an option, because Scheidemann, when proclaiming the German republic, had also declared that the new government under Ebert would be comprised

The revolutionary government – The "Council of People's Deputies", (right to left): Philipp Scheidemann (SPD), Wilhelm Dittmann (USPD), Hugo Haase (USPD), Friedrich Ebert (SPD), Otto Landsberg (SPD), and Emil Barth (USPD).

only of the two socialist parties, SPD and USPD. The following day, the revolutionary government, the "Council of the People's Deputies" (*Rat der Volksbeauftragten*) was established. This was a revolutionary government made up of three members of the SPD and another three of the USPD. The bourgeois heads of department still acted as administrative officials under the supervision of representatives of both Social Democratic parties. In the evening of 10 November, the revolutionary government was confirmed by the assembly of the workers' and soldiers' councils.

The members of the revolutionary cabinet – Scheidemann once called it the "six-headed Reich chancellor" – were equal numerically but not in terms of their political impact. Ebert, who was responsible for domestic politics and military affairs, the core scopes of the cabinet, was *primus inter pares*: he chaired the cabinet meetings and was still treated as "chancellor", first and foremost by the ministerial bureaucracy.

As People's Deputy, Friedrich Ebert's politics were determined, on the one hand, by the legacy of the Kaiserreich and the impact of the lost war and, on the other, by his democratic self-conception, which remained his guideline for life. "The democratisation process is a vital necessity for the Reich and its people", he wrote on 2 November 1918. Thus, two essential problems had to be addressed. For one, the most immediate needs of the population had to be met and the looming economic collapse averted. Also, it was necessary to pave the way for democracy. A believer in reform and democracy, Ebert opposed a long-term dictatorial revolutionary regime, which the Independent Social Democrats in particular aimed for. Some of his contemporaries cited his local background as a reason for his politics of gradual transition. One of his party comrades later wrote about Ebert, "Being born in Baden, democratic ideas were in his blood. He repelled the concept of revolution." It must be left undecided whether this anti-revolutionary attitude was in fact typical for anyone from Baden. Indeed, Ebert was a revolutionary against his will. He wanted to achieve democracy by gradual change. By favouring reform he represented the vast majority of Social Democrats. The SPD saw itself as a revolutionary party in theory but not in practice. The party's programme sounded radically revolutionary, but the party itself was, to the contrary, rather reformist in principle. The Social Democrats did not have a plan at the ready to transform the Reich. Although power had fallen into Ebert's hands on 9 November 1918, he intended to play according to the democratic rules and create a broad consensus.

Furthermore, the revolutionary government did not work in a political vacuum. It had to face the manifold consequences and enormous burdens of the lost war and the adamant victorious powers. Ebert's revolutionary cabinet was not in a position to create an abstract prototype of the new state considering the circumstances. Above all, time was pressing.

More than four years of war and the mobilisation of all parts of society had deformed the social structure and deepened the class divide. Germany was depleted and its population demoralised. In order to stabilise the country, the tension between classes, which had grown during the war, had to be reduced and the torn society had to be internally pacified. Germany, a highly developed industrial society at the time, had already moved on from semi-parliamentarism by implementing the October reforms and was largely democratic in constitutional terms. Now the country had to gradually transform itself into a stable democratic constitutional state. The revolutionary government had to face one of the most complex and difficult situations in modern German history, or to quote Ebert, "difficulties no other highly developed country had ever faced before in the entire history of the world". Urgent problems demanded immediate decisions.

2 Liquidator of the Kaiserreich and Trustee of Political Power

> "[...] the Provisional Government entered into a very evil heritage. We literally were the liquidators of the old regime: All barns, all stores were empty, we were running out of supplies, our credit was damaged, the morale had sunk. We [...] have applied all our strength to overcoming the dangers and the misery of the transitional period. We have not forestalled the National Assembly. However, since time and hardship were pressing, we have tried to fulfil the most urgent demands of the workers."

With these remarks at the opening session of the National Assembly on 6 February 1919 in Weimar, Friedrich Ebert described the complex problems which had appeared from 9 November 1918 onwards. He saw the government as the liquidator of the old regime and as a trustee of political power, not merely on behalf of one class but of the entire nation. He stated: "As long as our people is not in a position to choose its own government, any government will be provisional." That was how Ebert defined the revolutionary government and its responsibility to pave the way for the smooth transition to a democratic constitutional system. In order to achieve this goal, it was necessary to find vast support – even beyond the labour movement.

As early as 9 November, Ebert had urgently appealed to the administrative officers and civil servants to commit themselves to the service of the government in order to overcome the most pressing of problems such as "concluding an armistice and entering peace negotiations, securing food supplies for the people, enabling their comrades-in-arms to return as quickly and orderly as possible to their families and jobs". This one sentence comprised the key problems caused by the consequences of the war on which Ebert was particularly focused.

Securing food supplies was at the top of his list. The precarious food situation was one reason why the masses took to the streets in November 1918. After two winters of hunger and with the prospect of a third one with many further victims in sight, the discontented people demanded 'bread' in addition to 'peace and freedom'. Thus, the Council of the People's Deputies had to provide the population with 'bread'. The people would recognise the revolutionary government only if it succeeded in providing the necessary food supplies. Ebert's concern for food and energy was a common thread in his speeches during those weeks.

The basic circumstances were extremely bad: the Allies maintained a naval blockade and prevented the German fishing fleet from departing. Germany relied on concessions by the victorious Allies. Only food imports could secure the supplies of the population. By 1918/19, Ebert described the situation as extremely bleak and predicted the immediate collapse of all supplies. Securing food was closely linked to the issue of energy supply. "Do not disrupt coal mining", warned Ebert and Haase in one of the first proclamations of the revolutionary government on 11 November. The failure to maintain coal mining, at least to some degree (if not to increase it, as would have been necessary) would have had a negative impact on the food production.

The transition from a wartime to a peace economy was another difficulty to deal with. Three million workers in the arms-industry were affected. Almost 95 per cent of the entire industrial production was calibrated to war needs, Ebert noted worriedly in his diary on 21 November 1918. Now, that industry abruptly had to produce for a peace market. 'Pots' were needed from that point on, not 'grenades'. More than eight million soldiers returning from the theatres of war had to be provided with jobs and be reintegrated into an economy under substantial changes. All this exacerbated the difficulties.

The tense situation and these problems, which urgently needed to be resolved, were the main reason why the revolutionary government hesitated in the matter of socialising the major corporations – that is, converting them into public property. This had always been a key demand of Social Democracy. On 25 November, at the Conference of German States (*Länderkonferenz*), Ebert listed the factual reasons against the socialisation of the means of production as caused by the circumstances, "[...] at present, the productive resources are almost entirely exhausted, which makes it extremely difficult, even impossible, to put this [the socialisation] into practice. Therefore, it is vital to first provide our workers and soldiers returning from the front with jobs and the means to live". Moreover, Ebert wanted to create a vast consensus in favour of socialisation beyond the Social Democratic camp. For him, the future parliament had to decide on the basic issue of property rights and the order of property ownership, as he indicated to his co-members of the government in mid-November 1918: "We only want to socialise corporations which are ready to undergo this process. A committee of experts, with members also representing bourgeois parties – which will reassure everyone – shall assess the situation and decide in this matter. We want to avoid single experiments which could be potentially disturbing." Ebert queried whether it was wise to jeopardise the already tenuous food situation, caused by a dependence on a reliable coal supply, by converting the property rights of the coal mining industry, which was (or at least appeared to be) ready for nationalisation. "No experiments" was his guideline. The circumstances, he believed, only allowed for either an emergency pact or a structural reform, but not both of them. Bread and coal were urgently needed in the current situation, but structural reforms could be put on hold. Although Ebert did not mean to indefinitely postpone the reforms, they were indeed deferred.

Nothing was less welcome in this climate of economic crisis than strikes and industrial action. When trade unions and entrepreneurs' associations signed the so-called "Stinnes-Legien-Agreement" on 15 November (named after its chief negotiators the industrialist Hugo Stinnes and the union leader Carl Legien), Ebert believed that this step would set the course and provide much needed support. With the "Central Working Association Agreement" (*Zentralarbeitsgemeinschaftsabkommen*) employers committed themselves to recognising trade unions as (an equal) partner in labour relations. This defused the traditional differences between employers and employees, at least for the time being.

Given the accumulated problems at the end of the lost war (which Ebert never stopped mentioning), there was no leeway to change the personnel of the existing administration. For him the urgent call for action at that time of crisis made it imperative to rely on the more experienced personnel. Ebert pointed out at the Conference of German States:

> "After we had taken over political power, we had to make sure that the state machinery did not collapse [...], we had to make sure that the state machinery kept on going to maintain our food supply and our economy. [...] And that was not easy. With the utmost effort we have worked by day and by night in order to prevent the collapse and the downfall. [...] It was impossible for us six men to do that on our own. We needed the support of knowledgeable experts."

Considering the precarious internal situation and the external predicaments, Ebert believed that he had to draw on the traditional and still intact pre-revolutionary civil and military apparatuses. Thus, on 10 November 1918, Ebert talked over the phone to General Wilhelm Groener, First Quartermaster General of the Supreme Army Command (*Oberste Heeresleitung*; OHL), the highest military command centre. They came to an understanding on cooperation. Groener, a key figure within the OHL alongside the Supreme Commander Paul von Hindenburg, guaranteed the support of the military command centre for the new government. In return, the OHL expected the chain of command to be maintained. Ebert welcomed the willingness of the OHL to cooperate in this particular situation, without, however, making any political concessions. The agreement was no conspiratorial "pact" between Ebert and the traditional military powers, as it was later suggested. The agreement between the political and military leadership was nothing more than an act of political convenience and was meant to stabilise the governmental responsibility Ebert had just taken over. According to the conditions of the armistice treaty of 11 November, the German troops, still deep in enemy country, had to return to the Reich within 15 days. Ebert believed that this would require an efficient military organisation.

Neither regarding the cooperation with the old military elites nor in other areas did the Council of People's Deputies

The People's Representative Friedrich Ebert (centre), across from him Philipp Scheidemann, to his right Hugo Haase at the funeral of the victims of the revolution of 20 November. Their faces show the cumulative strain of wartime in its final weeks, the signing of the armistice, and revolution.

make any attempt at a fresh start in terms of personnel. It did not take into account that substituting the most compromised groups in core areas could have had symbolic character. Wiping the slate would have given a clear signal. It was due to their main concern regarding a functioning state as well as the economic and social consolidation that the People's Deputies did not make any personnel changes. "A failure of the organisation [...] would turn Germany into anarchy and terrible misery", the new chancellor Ebert had already warned on 9 November. That was why the Social Democratic government declined to change the personnel of the supreme authorities but urged the former imperial civil servants and officials to put themselves to the service of democracy and the new government.

3 Paving the Way for Democracy

Despite the focus on a functioning administration due to the problems at the time, the revolutionary government succeeded in carrying out groundbreaking reforms. On 12 November the People's Deputies implemented several Social Democratic demands in a proclamation. This constitutional document – which went down in history as the "Magna Carta of the German Revolution" – guaranteed fundamental rights such as the rights of association and of assembly as well as the rights of freedom of expression and of religion. Several further social political measures were initiated in addition to amendment regulations such as the abrogation of the state of siege which restricted civil rights and liberties, the amnesty of political offences and the re-enactment of regulations for the protection of workers, which had been repealed at the beginning of the war. This included the introduction by law of the eight-hour work day on 1 January 1919, the key political demand of the pre-war labour movement. The revolutionary government also introduced women's suffrage and laid the foundation for the political equality of men and women, which was a historical milestone. From now on, equal, secret, and direct suffrage applied to every citizen over the age of 20. At the same time, a system of proportional representation was introduced in lieu of the absolute majority voting system, which had put the SPD at a disadvantage during the Kaiserreich.

These impressive reforms paved the way for democracy, which was supposed to be enacted as soon as possible. Ebert's immediate goal was the National Assembly. He declared it "the holiest duty" to create a constitutional basis for the new republic and to convene a National Assembly the earliest possible date: "I am convinced: The legislative assembly is a bare necessity for Germany." At the end of November, he could rightly point out to the revolutionary cabinet that the overall majority of the people would demand the Constituent Assembly. Whilst the SPD, led by Ebert, championed the implementation of the new national parliament as soon as possible, the USPD had strong reservations against an early election date. The Independent Social Democrats wanted to carry out extensive reforms first and then to let the people decide. Ebert, on the other hand, had an unshakeable belief in the ballot. Thus, he wanted the National Assembly to take the basic decisions regarding constitutional and social policy issues.

As a representative of the Social Democrats, who had been socially excluded during the Kaiserreich, Ebert did not aspire to a new class rule. "All power to the councils", the rule which a particular class made up of a minority of revolutionaries around the radical Spartacus League – led by Rosa Luxemburg and Karl Liebknecht – demanded, was incompatible with Ebert's democratic convictions. Unlike the Kaiserreich, which was swept away by the revolution, the new republic was supposed to offer political participation to all segments of the

Friedrich Ebert welcomes the troops returning home from the front in the name of the revolutionary government at the Brandenburg Gate in Berlin on 10 December 1918.

population. This was Ebert's understanding of democracy. For him it was about equality of all people, the "great, ideal concept of democracy", as he put it in his introductory speech at the First General Conference of the Workers' and Soldiers' Councils of Germany on 16 December 1918:

> "There can only be one source of law in Germany in the long run: the will of the entire German people. That was the purpose of the revolution. [...] The victorious proletariat does not implement class rule. It overcomes the old system of class rule,

first in political, then in economic terms and establishes equality of all beings with a human face. That is the grand idea of democracy."

The Central Workers' and Soldiers' Councils Congress, which was in session in Berlin from 16 to 21 December 1918, had to decide on the date of the elections for the National Assembly. By that point it had become clear that a political system such as a Soviet republic or even a Soviet dictatorship was not on the agenda of the councils. The vast majority of the workers' and soldiers' councils founded during November 1918 regarded themselves as an executive body of the revolutionary government and supported the political programme of the Majority Social Democrats, which was based on parliamentary democracy and early elections for the National Assembly. With an overwhelming majority of around 400 votes in favour and only 50 votes against, the delegates resolved to hold elections for the National Assembly on 19 January 1919 – quite to Ebert's liking. The radicals' motion to maintain a system of councils as the foundation of the future German constitution, on the other hand, was not passed at the conference. 344 delegates voted against the resolution and merely 98 for it. Thus, nothing seemed to stand in the way of the first general elections.

However, the internal situation worsened. The political conflict spilled onto the streets after the Independent Social Democrats pulled out of the Council of the People's Deputies at the end of December 1918. They did so in protest to Ebert's decision to deploy military troops to quell the mutiny of the so-called *Volksmarinedivision* which had restrained Otto Wels (SPD), the military Town Commander for Berlin, and occupied the castle and the royal stables. For the three Independent People's Deputies, Ebert's course of action was only a pretext for pulling out of the government. The underlying cause for this lay in the increasing difficulties, first and foremost on military policy matters, between SPD and USPD due to the latter being put under increasing pressure by the radical left.

The decision of the Independent Social Democrats to pull out of the revolutionary government, henceforth comprised of only SPD representatives, directly led to the unrest in January, which were widely known as the Spartacist rebellion (*Spartakus-Aufstand*). It was an attempt by the radical left to bring down the "Ebert-Scheidemann government". They were organised by the new Communist Party of Germany (*Kommunistische Partei Deutschlands*; KPD), which had been founded on 1 January 1919 and was led by Karl Liebknecht. At that time the new People's Deputy Gustav Noske (SPD) took over supreme command of the army. Over the course of the increasingly escalating conflict it became clear that the revolutionary government not building up an army committed to the new democratic order after the revolution had been a mistake. The workers' and soldiers' councils had passed a programme of military reforms at the Reich Congress, which, however, the revolutionary government never implemented. Initially Ebert had suggested the establishment of a voluntary militia, but the Supreme Army Command (OHL) entrusted with this project did not pursue the matter further after the adoption of a law on that issue on 6 December 1918. Events overtook the planning.

In utmost distress, the Social Democratic revolutionary government drew on the traditional military elites and cemented the role of the Supreme Army Command as a political force. The military leadership primarily deployed right-wing militias (the so-called *Freikorps*) comprised mainly of demobilised soldiers who opposed democracy. The Freikorps had been hastily established in order to protect the Eastern border against Polish attacks. They quelled the riot within a few days. Even though the reckless course of action adopted by the government troops against the putschists met with justifiable criticism, it was an undeniable fact that the government had to take military action against the rebels in order to keep the door open to a republican system. The radicals threatened to destroy the path to free elections and thus to parliamentary democracy, that is to say everything Ebert had fought for his entire life.

The January uprising, its quelling by right-wing Freikorps, and the brutal killings of Rosa Luxemburg and Karl Liebknecht, both leaders of the Communist Party, by members of the Guards Riflemen Cavalry Division (*Garde-Schützen-Kavallerie-Division*) two days after the fighting, deepened the divide within the labour movement. These events and the failure to implement traditional Social Democratic reforms contributed to the radicalisation of the workers. The country was ravaged by strikes and civil war-like unrest in the spring of 1919. The second wave of the revolution became much more violent than the first one, which had begun on 9 November 1918. Again, Noske, supported by Ebert, proved to be a politician with an iron fist.

Despite the events during the months of the revolution, it must have been to Friedrich Ebert's great satisfaction to open the first parliament in German history based on free, secret, and general elections on 6 February 1919 in Weimar, the city to which the government had relocated the National Assembly due to the unrest in the capital of the Reich, not even 90 days after the collapse of the old regime and Ebert's take over as chancellor. Had he taken stock in February 1919, Friedrich Ebert might have seen more positives than negatives. Not only a long-lasting civil war but also the looming occupation by the victorious Allied Powers had been averted. The return of the troops and the process of their demobilization were as successful as their reintegration into industrial production. Food supplies for the population could be maintained despite the limited scope of possibilities. The state machinery functioned and the territorial integrity of the

Reich was preserved despite separatist currents rekindling time and again.

The fact that Ebert and his party, the (Majority) Social Democrats, did not make any attempts to democratise administration, economy, and military is one of the basic compromises which many contemporaries then and historians today think were more concessive than they had to be. According to this reproach, Ebert and the revolutionary government did not make use of the opportunity to establish a necessary and fundamentally new order. At the core of the debate among historians is the question of whether this was a missed opportunity to stabilise the foundation of the new republic. Critics reproach Ebert for not taking advantage of the potential for democratisation among the workers' and soldiers' councils in order to conduct structural reforms and changes of personnel. Indeed, Ebert did not consider the workers' and soldiers' councils as a power factor in the interplay of political forces. On the contrary, he saw them as more of a hindrance to the resolution of the existing problems and complained about their "meddling and interfering". He only accepted the workers' and soldiers' councils as temporarily required auxiliary bodies for the transitional period, although they would be dissolved as soon as democratic federal and state governments had been established.

Critics usually point out the lost opportunities. This, however, ignores what had been accomplished only a few weeks after the changes of 9 November 1918 and – of equal importance – what had been averted. There were not only (allegedly) missed chances, but also prevented disasters. It was to Ebert's credit and the achievements of the revolutionary government that a parliamentary democracy could have been created and established after such short a time given the circumstances, the basic conditions, and the overload of problems. Ebert and the SPD held onto their main political objective: Germany's permanent parliamentarisation and liberalisation. They strove for a broad consensus among the society by involving the reform-oriented bourgeois parties.

When assessing the politics of Ebert and the revolutionary government, the extreme pressure of time has to be taken into consideration. Additionally, the decision-makers had to face enormous physical and emotional strains. The political scene had become a boiling pot in which one had to have, in Philipp Scheidemann's words, "skin like a rhinocerous". Certainly, Ebert was thick-skinned. Yet he, too, had to fear for life and limb during those days. The revolutionary left increasingly mobilised their supporters, and their verbal radicalism was on the verge of turning into action. That probably affected Ebert. He believed that the way to democracy was threatened. Without a doubt, he overestimated the "Bolshevik threat" posed by the radical left. However, it was possible that even minorities could seize power. The Russian development was a cautionary tale for Ebert. There, the outnumbered Bolsheviks had neutralised the majority. That had caused a civil war with disastrous consequences – famine, widespread death, and economic chaos that tore the country apart. Germany should be spared such a situation.

By means of the revolution, Ebert had achieved his main objective: implementing parliamentary democracy. Anything else would have been undemocratic, according to his view, because it was not based on the verdict of the electorate. The reproach of not having undertaken particular reforms did not hit the convinced democrat Ebert since he regarded all these reforms – which are considered necessary for a long lasting democracy – as a task of the future parliament. It is arguable whether Ebert's policies were right or wrong but they were by no means undemocratic, and they in no way represented a betrayal of his party's principles. Although Ebert, whose political guiding principle was the will of the electorate, strongly believed that the republic could only survive on the basis of a class compromise between the Social

Democratic labour movement and the democratic bourgeoisie, he was unable to adopt a course fundamentally different to the one adopted in the three months following the revolution of 9 November 1918. There was no democratic alternative to the politics of Ebert and the (Majority) Social Democrats.

The foundation of a political reorganisation was laid and the republic founded. From then on, it was the task of the constitutional National Assembly to elaborate and secure parliamentary democracy. From that point on, Friedrich Ebert's main concern became enshrining the achievements of the revolution in a democratic constitution which placed all power in the hands of the people. The people, the highest sovereign in a democratic system, had given its verdict on 19 January 1919. The first democratic parliament in Germany had to decide on future developments. This was the fundamental principle to which Ebert felt committed – even beyond the revolutionary period.

IV Head of State in the Weimar Republic (1919–1925)

1 A President for every German

In 1919, the first Reich President Friedrich Ebert offered his mission statement for his tenure at the summit of the first German republic: "Carried by my unwavering belief in the creativity of the German people, I want to commit my all for the protection of the democracy and the rebuilding of our economic life." Ebert's politics during the revolution were oriented towards compromise, be it between the Social Democratic labour movement and the democratic bourgeoisie, between reorganisation and conservation, or, not to be overlooked, between the federal state and constituent states. This remained his objective once he was elected president.

Ebert had sought the highest public office even before the elections for the National Assembly. In his view, the head of state had to play an active and participatory role. Additionally, he recognised the post's high potential for integration. When the revolutionary government, the Council of the People's Deputies, discussed the draft constitution, Ebert criticised the extensive powers of the future Reich president, who was to be elected to office by the people, as being too far reaching. Nevertheless, he ultimately accepted the post and its responsibilities. As a sober and rational politician, he had no doubt that "certain powers" were essential for a "united and powerful leadership of the country", as he highlighted during a meeting of the revolutionary cabinet in the midst of January 1919.

As president, Ebert wanted to take the opportunity to forge the alliance between Social Democratic labour movement and democratic bourgeoisie as well as overcome the social divide between "*Reichstreuen*" (loyalists to the defunct

A "cheer" for the first democratically elected head of state in front of the Weimar theatre after Friedrich Ebert's election as president 11 February 1919.

Empire) and the "*vaterlandslose Gesellen*" (the "men without a fatherland") which had characterised the Kaiserreich. During the negotiations for the formation of the first republican government he therefore relied on the so-called Weimar Coalition composed of SPD, Catholic Centre Party (*Zentrum*; Z), and left liberal DDP (*Deutsche Demokratische Partei*; German Democratic Party). A coalition with the USPD was out of the question for Ebert after his bitter experience during the revolutionary period. Besides, the two Social Democratic parties did not have a majority in the National Assembly. The alliance of the SPD with the two bourgeois republican parties established by Philipp Scheidemann, co-leader of the SPD, held a comfortable three-quarter majority. By forming such a broad coalition in addition to a Social Democratic president, a truly powerful republican state leadership had been accomplished. However, the coalition failed after only a few months. It collapsed in June 1919 amidst differences over the peace treaty. Although the alliance was renewed in October 1919, it never attained the strength that Ebert had hoped for.

These events were already in the offing when Ebert was elected as president. On 6 February 1919, he inaugurated the National Assembly saying: "The people of Germany are free, remain free, and will only be governed by themselves." Five days later, the parliament elected the Social Democrat Ebert as the first democratic head of state in German history by 277 of 379 votes. The result was not as strong as expected, since more than 50 representatives of the prospective Weimar Coalition did not vote for Ebert, although he had paved the way during the negotiations on forming a government. Nevertheless, the election of the Social Democrat Friedrich Ebert, once excluded as an enemy of the Reich, to the highest public office of the new republic was a clear sign of a new constitutional beginning.

After his election, Ebert pledged that he would represent the entire German people and not simply act as the "leader of any single party". This commitment to non-partisanism remained his guiding principle during his term as head of state. He also promised "to protect the freedom of all Germans with all my power and my full dedication. That is the oath I take in this moment, and that I put in the hands of the National Assembly". While the interests of state and those of his party tore Ebert in different directions, he presided for six years as head of state, over a widely unpopular republic, beset from abroad, and internally at odds with itself.

He appeared willing to use the power of the office consistently. The "*Act on Provisional Power in the Reich*" (*Gesetz über die vorläufige Reichsgewalt*) from 10 February 1919, the transitional constitution, already showed the outlines of the later presidential power. They were ultimately codified in the national constitution passed by the National Assembly at the end of July 1919. The fact that, according to the constitution of Weimar, the president had to be elected directly by the people for a seven-year term, gave the office more power than any other institution in the republic. However, Ebert was never elected by the people. Although he had always pressed for the holding of elections, the government hesitated. Finally, on 24 October 1922, the Reichstag prolonged his term in office until 30 June 1925 by a constitutional amendment. Even though he was never elected directly by the people – which caused some defamatory attacks such as calling him "Friedrich the Provisional" – Ebert saw himself as a full-fledged president.

The constitution had created a head of state with considerable power. The president had the right to appoint the chancellor, could dissolve the Reichstag, and could issue emergency decrees in accordance with the government without the approval of parliament. In addition, he was the foreign policy representative of the Reich and the supreme commander of the armed forces. Compared to government and parliament, his position was extremely powerful – at least according to constitutional theory. Yet in contrast to the intentions of the authors of the constitution and their concept of a powerful president, directly elected by the people and as a counterbalance to parliament and the cabinet, the first republican head of state always saw himself as a part of, and not an adversary to the government. The unity of the government was an invariable rule for Ebert. Given the situation of permanent crisis, he warned in a cabinet meeting in 1921 that "the leadership must be firmly kept in the government's hands". Conflicts should be resolved internally. That was Ebert's first political principle, a conviction originating from the time before the First World War, when the Social Democrats wasted much of their political strength by holding philosophical debates in public. According to his guideline, controversial issues should be discussed behind closed doors, and after having agreed on a compromise, all parties involved had to publicly advocate the consensus with one voice. He

Friedrich and Louise Ebert during their holidays in Schwarzburg 1919.

followed this principle during his time as party leader and even more when he was president.

However, that did not mean that government and president were in perfect harmony with each other. The president did not shy away from conflicts with the government and insisted on his rights. In the cabinet, Ebert proved himself as a co-operative team player who knew how to stand his ground and when to accept the opinion of the majority. In some cases he would have done better if he had insisted on his view more strongly. For instance, he did not want to approve the extremely moderate court-martial decision against the murderers of Rosa Luxemburg and Karl Liebknecht, which many regarded as scandalous. Instead, his intention was to reopen the proceedings. However, he acquiesced to the majority of the cabinet. Subsequently, Gustav Noske (SPD), the responsible minister of defence, confirmed the verdicts, squandering the opportunity to serve justice.

Similarly, Ebert failed to pursue a campaign of honestly considering the question of war-guilt vigorously enough. He himself had demanded that the campaign be conducted. It would have eased the burden for the republican government if an inquiry of the events of 1914 had shown that the old imperial regime had been primarily responsible for the outbreak of the war. Ebert was convinced that Germany had to bear the lion's share of the blame. However, he did not accept the notion that Germany was solely responsible for the war, as it was put in the Treaty of Versailles. The new decision-makers admitting Germany's responsibility for the outbreak of the war would have shown the new republic's break with the Kaiserreich and the condemnation of its monarchist politics of striving for power. Ebert recognised this opportunity. However, he did not insist on or publicly demand the repudiation of the Wilhelmine foreign policy on the part of the democratic government. In this point, he followed the majority instead of standing his ground and taking the lead.

Ebert, always anxious to reach a consensus, acted as an intermediary and mediator, as a man of compromise and balance in contentious debates. Those who met the president in person or had a conversation with him in private, enjoying one of his usual morning cigars in his smoke-filled office in the Berlin Palais at 73 Wilhelmstraße, came to know his warmth and his modest endearing manner. The day after Ebert's election, the publicist Theodor Wolff wrote in the "*Berliner Tageblatt*":

> "In his youth committed to the saddler's craft, Fritz Ebert is now ascending to the throne […] Admittedly, Ebert represents neither the highest form of cultural refinement nor the most outstanding of statesmanship. Yet he has endearing and invaluable qualities, first and foremost among them a down-to-earth warmth and a deep honesty. He is not a radiant genius […] but he personifies what one might call good judgment."

There was never a consensus opinion regarding Ebert, be it the man or the politician. This holds true not only for the German public, but also for the diplomats who came into contact with the first president. The American envoy Ellis Loring Dresel wrote that Ebert, whom he met while travelling through Germany at the turn of the year 1918, was a man of "great honesty and sincerity". From the earliest days of the revolution, the Americans considered Ebert to be "entirely sincere and truthful". The American ambassador Alanson B. Houghton, who had been appointed in 1922, noted in his diary in early 1925: "Ebert is really a remarkable figure. To me, he is the strongest and ablest German I have met."

Sir Edgar Vincent Baron D'Abernon, the British ambassador to Germany since 1920, employed a tone far-removed from that of his American counterpart, an industrialist from Corning, New York. D'Abernon, a man from a very different social background to Ebert's, officer of his Majesty and long-term representative in the House of Commons, could not find much common ground with Ebert, and he let this social disparity bleed into his assessment:

> "The Reichs Präsident, Ebert, was there, and I had some conversation with him after dinner. One never sees him without wondering whether he is not really the Mayor of some small French town near Besançon. Little of the German about him; nothing of the Socialist; and less of the working saddler. He looks as if he had been in the enjoyment of a small bourgeois business since the day he was born. Those who come into close contact with him say he is sensible and clear-headed, but I have formed no special liking for him myself."

Nevertheless, he also saw himself compelled to amend his opinion, even though he did not want to distance himself much from his earlier judgement. Following a reception in January 1924, he noted:

> "Considering he was a working saddler and that she (Ebert's wife) began life in very humble circumstances, it is astonishing with what dignity and reserve they behave. Nobody would take a liberty with Ebert; even with the most aristocratic of the former Princes and princelings he would maintain his composture. One cannot say that he is agreeable, but he converses easily and with extreme good sense. Nothing original, but nothing false."

The prudent negotiator Ebert was always asked when the situation seemed to be hopeless. Often, he was able to break the ice. Even though he usually stoically balanced the different interests, he could get upset. Chancellor Joseph Wirth later characterised him as "vibrant and easily irritable, typical for someone from the Palatinate". Is there a chance that Wirth, a member of the Centre Party and born in Baden, had indeed identified a typical Palatine trait? In any event, it is well documented that the Heidelberg-born Ebert could sometimes react rather gruffly.

Yet, he was also able to listen to reason and amend his opinion if he was convinced by counter arguments. He was far away from being dogmatic or self-righteous. On the other hand, he never turned into the compliant henchman of the government. Overall, he was actively involved in politics – to an even higher degree than was publicly known – and fulfilled his task meticulously. He was neither willing nor able to act as a substitute emperor by interfering extensively in politics. He rather saw his role as that of protector of the constitution and keeper of democratic order. Friedrich Ebert used the powers of the presidency to the fullest, and, in doing so, he developed the highest public office, for which no previous example existed, into a powerful institution within the domestic political constellation of the young republic. By no means did he wither into a paper tiger, with mere representative function. Ebert was and remained an active president.

All his actions followed the objective of securing a functioning parliamentary system.

2 President and Government

One of the key tasks of the Reich president was to appoint the chancellor (*Reichskanzler*). Ebert did not regard this merely as a formal procedure, but as a chance for participation. During the discussions about the formation of the government he acted on the conviction that – given the social disarray caused by the consequences of the war – permanent stability was possible only if the new democratic system was capable of relieving tensions between classes and pacifying the fractured society. In his view the republic was only viable through the cooperation between working class and bourgeoisie. In order to overcome the apparently overwhelming obligations to the victorious powers and the internal strain caused by them, Ebert considered it necessary to incorporate industrial interests to the aforementioned cooperation between the classes. The burden had to be shared by many. On the basis of this assessment, Ebert urged his party to enter into a government alliance with the constitutional bourgeois parties time and again. That also included the right-wing liberal German People's Party (*Deutsche Volkspartei*; DVP) under the leadership of Gustav Stresemann which had changed sides and become "rational republicans" (so-called *Vernunftrepublikaner*) in the middle of 1920. Friedrich Ebert sought as broad a government as possible in order to work in the long term. But that was just wishful thinking.

Ebert first called for a grand coalition between SPD, Centre Party, DDP, and DVP after the Reichstag elections in June 1920, when the Weimar Coalition forfeited its majority and the Social Democrats lost a dramatic amount of votes.

The feast in commemoration of the 10th anniversary of the outbreak of the First World War on 3 August 1924 is more than a mere official appearance for Friedrich Ebert, who had lost two of his own sons on the battlefield. The photograph shows Friedrich Ebert with three chancellors: the then serving Wilhelm Marx (second from the left), his predecessor Gustav Stresemann (sixth from the right), and Hans Luther (left of Ebert), who later became head of government in January 1925.

In November 1922, he addressed party representatives saying, "I have never concealed that I resolutely champion the concept of a grand coalition, perhaps born out of a political need, but for the good of the state."

He promoted his view that compromise between interest groups and parties was an integral part of parliamentary democracy, and that the current tense situation in particular required a broad consensus. The parties, however, were in many cases not prepared to follow this principle, because they lacked the will to compromise in order to combine very different interests. Ebert, on the other hand, thought it possible to overcome the ideological and programmatic obstacles between the parties. He always expected that the parties would subordinate their tactical aims to the abstract "good of the state". Time and again he preached reason, advocated unity and a cohesive "phalanx" in order to deal with the consequences of the Treaty of Versailles. Yet this was prevented by the political camp's segmentation into a plethora of different parties. Furthermore, the lack of governing experience under the factual constraints of a coalition, which was due to the established parties being excluded from actual political participation in the Kaiserreich, proved yet another obstacle to Ebert's strides towards parliamentary unity. They had never learned how to form a parliamentary government. The parties preferred to return to their comfortable opposition seats. It did not help either that voters in Weimar often punished the parties which took part in government.

Thus, the SPD reacted to the poor result in the first Reichstag elections in June 1920 (21.7 per cent, compared to 37.9 per cent in the elections for the National Assembly in January 1919) by going into opposition. After being relieved of responsibility, the party intended to gather strength and try to win back voters who had changed to its more left-leaning rivals, the Independent Social Democrats. Ebert probably understood his party's reasoning. From a national political point of view, however, he did not appreciate the surrender of power, as the power politician disapproved of any government hastily throwing in the towel. The enormous obligations to the Allies and the profound decisions they required had caused more than one politician to quit. Ebert must have been quite disconcerted when Constantin Fehrenbach of the Centre Party resigned in May 1921, just a few weeks before the Allies' London ultimatum was to expire, demanding the German acceptance of the reparations claims. It had taken weeks of negotiation before all of the parties agreed on Fehrenbach as chancellor at the end of June 1920. By resigning, Fehrenbach caused a crisis of government at the worst of all times.

In 1922, Ebert told some party friends in Dessau that the Social Democrats had learned to "be there when they were asked to". He acted on this principle and expected others mainly, but not exclusively, from his party to do so as well. He was impressed by the new Chancellor Joseph Wirth from the Centre Party who decisively addressed looming issues in May 1921, and overcame a political crisis in October 1921 in the wake of the Allies' decision to divide Upper Silesia by acting decisively and quickly forming a new cabinet.

Several attempts to form a government developed into a deadlocked situation, because the parties hesitated and did not decisively take power, such as in June 1920. Ebert ultimately pressured the Centre Party until Constantin Fehrenbach accepted the office of chancellor. Some candidates, whom Ebert had initially favoured, failed during the first steps of negotiations due to the stubborn attitude of the parties involved. Some politicians persuaded by Ebert to campaign fell victim to the infighting between opposing wings of their own party.

The president found it difficult to find suitable candidates who were willing and capable to form a sustainable government due to the politicians' habit of escaping responsibility. The satirical magazine "*Simplicissimus*" published a caricature in 1923 depicting Ebert restlessly tossing in bed, under the title, "The never-ending chancellor crisis", subtitled with a quote by the poet Heinrich Heine from 1843, "Thinking of Germany in the night just puts all thoughts of sleep to flight". Indeed, the question of chancellorship probably robbed Ebert of sleep at times. He often had to put massive pressure on the candidate he favoured – sometimes even threatening to resign – in order to persuade the politician in question to take over government. Some attempts to form a government developed into an unpleasant walk on eggshells. They were dominated by tactical manoeuvring, much to Ebert's disapproval. In his mind such manoeuvring damaged the reputation of parliamentary democracy. In some deadlocked situations the president did not hesitate to use unconventional methods. In 1924 he twice dissolved the Reichstag in accordance with the government and large parts of parliament, because it was no longer possible to govern due to the entrenched positions. However, after the election there were again no clearly defined majorities. Once again it took a long time until the governments were established.

In November 1922, when the Wirth government failed, the parties did not make any effort to nominate a chancellor or to enter into government. In this situation of political numbness, Ebert appointed Wilhelm Cuno, a conservative without party affiliations and director of the Hamburg-based Hapag shipping company, as head of the so-called "*Geschäftsministerium*", a nonpartisan cabinet composed of independent experts. Appointing Cuno as chancellor illustrated the crisis of the parliamentary party state. Later, the appointment turned out to be a mistake, as Cuno, a highly regarded economic expert, and his team proved incapable of handling the worsening internal and external situations in view of the French-Belgian occupation of the Ruhr and the dramatically growing inflation.

Ebert's desired coalition came into being in summer 1923, just as Germany was on the brink of collapse. Yet the "Grand Coalition", ranging from DVP to SPD, under Chancellor Gustav Stresemann (DVP) did not even last three months – very much to Ebert's annoyance. Finally, and after strong appeals he persuaded Wilhelm Marx (Centre Party), who initially was hesitant, to take over chancellorship. This was another instance in which the president profoundly influenced the question of who would become the next chancellor, as he had done at the beginning of his term in office. In June 1919, Ebert had appointed his closest friend Gustav Bauer (SPD) as head of government – against the intentions of the SPD parliamentary group, which favoured the party leader

Long-time companions, linked by a close friendship: Friedrich and Louise Ebert in Schwarzburg (Thuringia) with Gustav Bauer, appointed chancellor in June of 1919, and his wife Hedwig.

Hermann Müller, who indeed succeeded Bauer in March 1920.

By the end of the year 1924, Ebert realised that the president's influence on the negotiations regarding the formation of a government was limited if the parties acted single-mindedly. For instance, he fought vigorously against the participation of the anti-republican DNVP in the government, which was adamantly championed by Stresemann in autumn 1924. In early 1925, after months of fighting, Ebert had to give in and dismiss Marx, to whom he had wanted to hold on by all means in order to prevent a strong shift to the right. It was under the new independent Chancellor Hans Luther that members of the anti-democratic DVNP, which had declared a political war on the republic, first joined the government. Among them was a minister who, as a civil servant, had refused to take the oath to the constitution in 1920. Ebert probably considered it an aberration that, of all politicians, it had to be a member of the DNVP who became minister of the interior and thus head of the department responsible for constitutional issues. Though that might have gone against the grain for him, Ebert could not prevent it from happening. The president's influence on choosing the chancellor and forming a coalition government was therefore limited if the parties were active. They, however, often hesitated to take responsibility.

During the six years of his term, the first president saw no fewer than nine chancellors and more than a dozen cabinets, most of them not even holding a majority in parliament. The average government did not last longer than six months. Compared to that, the six years of Ebert's term in office were remarkable. By 1925 he was in many respects the last of the Mohicans – those who had come into office in 1918/19 and still held their post. Ebert himself often wished to relieve himself of the burden of the office after experiencing the situations of permanent crisis during the first years of the Weimar Republic, which first occurred when he had to decide on whether to accept the peace treaty.

3 Foreign Policy Representative of the Reich

Signing the Treaty of Versailles was the young republic's first foreign policy challenge. The first draft of the treaty published by the Allies in the beginning of May 1919 was quite a blow for the defeated German Reich. Before the conditions of the treaty became known, Ebert had hoped for a "peace of understanding and reconciliation". This expectation proved to be illusory. After the treaty drafted by the Allies had been published, hopes for a bearable peace made way for indignation. In addition to surrendering a seventh of the territory of the Reich, the loss of the colonies and a drastic reduction of the armed forces, it was first and foremost the so-called infamous article 231 (*Schmachartikel*) that caused outrage. The treaty established high, although not yet specified reparation payments, which were justified by the victorious powers on the grounds of Germany's sole responsibility for causing the war. Philipp Scheidemann summarised the general mood when addressing the National Assembly on 12 May: "What hand would not wither which binds itself, and us, in these fetters?" Ebert did not remain unaffected by Scheidemann's pithy words. A few days later, he coined the sentence: "We would have neither honour nor dignity, if we did not use all our strength against the disgrace which is threatening us."

It was one thing to publicly protest out of helpless rage, but another to rationally analyse the possibilities for recourse, and these were limited. Ultimately, Ebert was able to bring himself to sign the treaty. There was no alternative to accepting the peace treaty dictated by the victorious powers – unless Germany wanted to take on the risk of a new armed conflict without having a reasonable possibility to achieve victory against the Allies, who were in a superior military position. To paraphrase Ebert, their "strength" was not enough to fight the "disgrace". Given the fact that the Allies ultimately threatened to resume hostilities, the National Assembly had no choice at all but to accept the treaty, which they did immediately after the resignation of the Scheidemann cabinet on 23 June 1919. Ebert did all in his power to gather a majority in favour of the acceptance of the treaty before the Allied ultimatum expired. In the end, he succeeded in doing so.

Friedrich greets Mexican President-Elect Plutarco Elías Calles in Berlin, one of the few diplomatic events of international significance because of Germany's isolation.

In the face of the enormity of the decision, Ebert, like many other politicians during those dramatic days of June 1919, stood on the brink of a physical and emotional breakdown. He considered stepping down from his post, which was exactly how the government under Philipp Scheidemann reacted in opposition to the Treaty of Versailles. Ebert, on the other hand, was guided by the insight that his resignation would cause a national crisis of unforeseeable consequences for the existence of the Reich. Thus, he showed the high degree of ethics and responsibility which characterised him as president. His ability to persevere is even more significant given that other politicians divested themselves of the burden of their posts – an understandable reaction given their personal perspective, though it carried devastating consequences in terms of national politics.

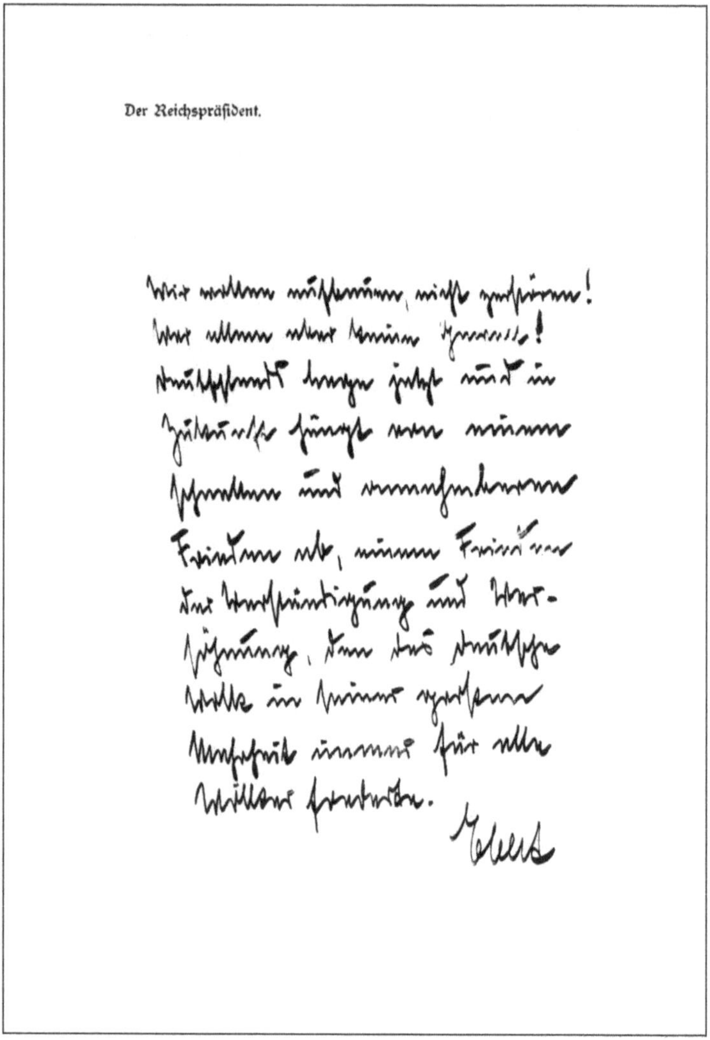
Der Reichspräsident.

Wir wollen aufbauen, nicht zerstören!
Wir wollen aber keinen Zwang!
Deutschland lehnt jetzt und in
Zukunft [illegible] von einem
[illegible] und [illegible]
Frieden ab, einen Frieden
der Verständigung und Ver-
söhnung, den das deutsche
Volk in seiner großen
Mehrheit immer für alle
Völker erstrebte.
Ebert

Handwritten note by Friedrich Ebert in 1919: hope for a "peace of understanding and reconciliation".

The peace treaty and the ensuing nationalist agitation against the "shameful peace of Versailles" (*Schandfrieden*) turned into a heavy burden for the Weimar Republic. Ebert was convinced that the liabilities could only be alleviated through persistent negotiations with the Western powers. His objective was to use the already existing manoeuvring room in foreign policy, even if it was marginal. On the basis of this insight he supported the so called "policy of fulfilment" (*Erfüllungspolitik*), according to which Germany would try to comply with the demands of the victorious powers only to prove that they were impossible to meet. Berlin hoped this would induce concessions from the Allies.

Given the important role of foreign affairs, Ebert wanted to participate in developing political concepts and implementing them. He knew that foreign policy decisions affected weal and woe of the republic in terms of domestic policy – first and foremost in its financial performance. Ebert left no doubt that he intended to take up the role of representative of the Reich according to international law, as assigned to him by article 45 of the constitution. Beyond the formal representation of the German Republic *vis-à-vis* other foreign states, the constitution granted him a factual authority to participate in the decision-making process. In addition to participating in foreign policy affairs, Ebert also intervened in issues of personnel and organisation, for instance, in the reorganisation of the Foreign Office (*Auswärtiges Amt*) and the diplomatic service. According to article 46 of the Reich constitution, the president was not only the foreign policy representative of the Reich but also had the right to appoint civil servants, thus being concerned with personnel policy. From this same constitutional article, Ebert also deduced the authority to co-decide on the appointment of a foreign minister whom he was able to trust. The chancellor could not appoint a foreign minister without, or against, the president. The appointment of several of the eight foreign ministers during Ebert's term in office was due to his initiative.

Ebert's choice of diplomatic personnel, ambassadors, and envoys was based on the intention to give a clear sign of constitutional change from the Kaiserreich to the republic. The majority of civil servants in the German Foreign Office had already served in the Kaiserreich and was not willing to completely break with old traditions, though quite a few of them had at least come to terms with the new system. Besides, Ebert conceded that some were doing excellent work. Thus, a substantial change of personnel in the Foreign Office did not seem advisable to him. He nevertheless attempted to appoint individuals from beyond the sphere of ministerial and diplomatic bureaucracy for posts in German embassies. During his term in office, the diplomatic service changed to a significant extent and became open to people from different professional backgrounds.

Ebert intervened in personnel policy as well as in issues of foreign policy representation. Here, however, the activities of the president remained limited. He did not take any trips abroad due to Germany's international isolation. Very few guests of state visited the Reich, which was why the government attached much importance to even quite insignificant diplomatic events. For instance, Ebert received Plutarco Elías Calles, the elected but not yet inaugurated Mexican president, as any other head of state. He also paid a visit to an Argentine training vessel, because the Foreign Office expected an increase in international prestige. The president's tasks as foreign policy representative were generally limited to receiving ambassadors for their accreditation and hosting the New Year's reception of the diplomatic corps, on which Ebert put special emphasis. Yet, he felt that the support of the Foreign Office in this matter was insufficient.

Disagreements with the Foreign Office in the matter of his role as foreign policy representative proved to be quite marginal compared to the substantial differences about the basic course of foreign policy. It remained Ebert's guideline to reduce the reparation payments and to reintegrate Germany into the community of nations of equal standing through constant negotiations with the Western Allies. Stamina was required in order to hold to this course. Hoping for concessions from the victors was quite an ordeal. Time and again, Ebert felt disappointed. "We are fully aware [...] that we must bear the cross alone and drain the chalice of sorrow to the dregs", the president, who was on the verge of resigning, said in November 1920.

When the Allies set the reparations terms in January 1921, according to which Germany had to pay 226 billion gold marks, Ebert's confidence dwindled completely. The chalice Germany had to drain was more than full. As many times before, Ebert summoned the "firm community of fate" of the German people. However, the cabinet of Chancellor Fehrenbach resigned, leaving the new government under Chancellor Wirth no choice but to accept the London Schedule of Payments and its harsh conditions.

Hardly half a year later the next blow followed with the Allies' decision on Upper Silesia. As mandated by the peace treaty, a border referendum was carried out in March 1921. Although the majority of the local population voted in favour of remaining within Germany, the Allies decided to partition the Prussian province between Poland and Germany. The German side, including Ebert, was extremely disappointed. The then chancellor Wirth remembered many years later, "I had never seen Ebert more devastated."

In April 1922, it was Chancellor Joseph Wirth and his foreign minister Walther Rathenau (DDP) who caused Ebert further disappointment by signing the treaty of Rapallo between Germany and Soviet Russia. The completion of the treaty in the Northern Italian city took the president by surprise. Wirth had gone to lengths to conceal the secretly conducted preparations from Ebert, knowing about the president's orientation toward the Western Allies and his distrust of the Soviets. The president did not want to negotiate with Moscow, as he did not consider the Bolsheviks trustworthy. But even Ebert did not categorically exclude the possibility of carefully approaching Soviet Russia if it proved necessary. He was politically realistic enough to keep an eye on German interests in the East. However, the Treaty of Rapallo was an unnecessary and ill-timed *tour de force* in his eyes.

The treaty, which established diplomatic relations between Germany and Soviet Russia, alienated Ebert for a long time due to his conviction that the new orientation to the East would profoundly damage his policy towards the West and Germany's relations to the Western powers. In addition to that, he as president – with his constitutional authority rights as foreign policy representative – felt taken by surprise and snubbed by what he considered a prematurely signed treaty. The Foreign Office, in its policy towards the East, had disregarded him once before. In May 1921, the government had signed two treaties with Soviet Russia in a *coup de main* manner. Ebert only learned about the hasty signing of the treaties from the newspapers. Joseph Wirth, who was finance minister at the time, had forced the conclusion of the treaties by pre-empting the head of state and dismissing his severe concerns about these compacts. The same happened one year later, with Wirth again as the key figure though this time acting as head of government.

Ebert was very much upset about the single-handed course of action of the chancellor and the foreign minister in Rapallo. He refused all attempts of appeasement on the part of others. However, even though the coup had caused an irreversible break between Ebert on the one hand and Wirth and Rathenau on the other, the president did not want to cause a governmental crisis. He did not give rise to any doubts that complete unity of the government had to be displayed in public. That way, he acted in accordance to his self-conception as pillar

Friedrich Ebert visits the Argentine ship *Presidente Sarmiento* in Hamburg with the Argentine envoy Louis Molina (right) in July 1923.

of the government. Showing unity was the maxim he acted on, despite his disappointment. Towards the press he championed the treaty as necessary and essential – contrary to his own judgement.

However, the relationship between president and chancellor was severely damaged —which was not inconsequential for Wirth's later failure. Due to the Rapallo treaty and other single-handed actions, Wirth had lost all his credibility in the eyes of the president. In November 1922, after the chancellor had driven the week-long negotiations on the enlargement of the coalition by the DVP under Stresemann into a dead end, Ebert did not do anything to hold onto the politically inept Centre Party politician. For a long time, the Reich president had appreciated Wirth as a decisive politician. In 1922, however, Wirth's failure was not to Ebert's inconvenience. Rapallo had been a serious blow.

Although the treaty was in fact a success for Germany in light of its internationally isolated situation, it caused, just as Ebert had feared, irritation among the Western powers. France took a swipe at Germany and occupied the Ruhr area in January 1923, which was followed by the most severe crisis of the republic. In this emergency situation, as in many others before, the president was in particular demand.

4 The President and the Crises of the Republic

The first years of the republic were characterised by local unrest rekindling time and again. The Kapp-Lüttwitz Putsch in March 1920 was the first attempt on a national level to bring down the young republic. It was triggered by the drastic demobilisation of the standing army, which still comprised 500,000 soldiers at the time, but was to be reduced to 100,000 according to the Treaty of Versailles. Ebert was, as commander-in-chief, actively engaged in matters concerning military personnel even more than it was known at the time, but he often relied on the expertise of high ranking military officers and politicians responsible for military policy. However, Ebert never turned into a compliant or ill-advised henchman. He only pursued those military policies which he considered to be necessary and possible. Neither structural reform, nor extensive changes in personnel had been initiated during the revolutionary period. Instead, Ebert made the preliminary decisions for the future army by resorting to working with the old military elites.

As Reich president, Ebert pursued his military policy. He intended to gradually build up a trusting relationship between the military and the Reich president without profound changes in personnel, or reorganising the basic structure. It was his aim to integrate those military officers who had begun their careers under the Kaiserreich into the republic and to offer them the opportunity to come to terms with the democratic system. Yet, the officer corps did not warrant his trust in them.

Over the course of the forced demobilisation of the Reichswehr in compliance with the Treaty of Versailles, the Marine Brigade Ehrhardt – the most effective corps of the Reich at the time – was one of the units to be dissolved in March 1920. General Walther von Lüttwitz called on Ebert to reverse the directive, issuing an ultimatum. Ebert refused. This was the signal for a right-wing militant group of conspirators around the high-ranking officials Wolfgang Kapp and General Lüttwitz to commence their attempted *coup d'état*.

During the first hours of the putsch on 13 March 1920, the fate of the legitimate government depended primarily on the reaction of the republic's military leaders. The majority of the officers responsible for the defence of the republic were not willing to stop the Marine Brigade Ehrhardt, which was advancing on Berlin, because – as they stated – the troops were incapable of dealing with the emotional impact of firing on their comrades. They believed in the slogan "Reichswehr never fires at Reichswehr". Walter Reinhardt, commander-in-chief of the army and therefore chief military officer of the Reich, was the sole advocate of the use of force against the putschists.

After being let down by the armed forces, the government's only choice was to escape. Ebert, accompanied by some of his ministers, fled from Berlin to Dresden, the capital of Saxony. Putschist troops marched into the Berlin government quarter only a few minutes later. In Dresden, Ebert and the government took their first countermeasures. However, Saxony soon became too dangerous for them. They moved on to the South of Germany until they reached Stuttgart, in Württemberg. Once he had arrived there, Ebert refused to make any concessions to the putschists: "No negotiations

With Minister of Defence Gustav Noske (left) and General Wilhelm Groener (right) in Schwarzburg in late July 1919, discussing military policy.

with Kapp and his comrades." After a few days, everything was over. It was primarily the national strike of the labour movement which ended the putsch attempt, because" all wheels came to a halt". The government had scarcely fled from Berlin, when a general strike – endorsed by the ministers of the SPD and Reich president Ebert – was called. In the end, the general strike brought the coup to its knees. Fully aware of their success, large factions of the SPD and trade unions demanded the dismissal of Gustav Noske, Minister of Defence (*Reichswehrminister*), whom they held responsible for the republic's failed military policy. Ebert, however, held onto the controversial Social Democratic minister. He was convinced that Noske was the only person capable of controlling the Reichswehr. In addition, he feared that the SPD would lose the important ministry to another party if Noske were to resign. Nevertheless, Ebert was ultimately forced to bow to the pressure from his own ranks. Since there was no Social Democratic candidate found for the unpopular post, the party lost this key bastion, as Ebert had correctly predicted and, along with it, the chance of having an impact on the Reichswehr in order to turn it into a pro-republican instrument of power. Out of solidarity with Noske, Reinhardt submitted his final resignation as well. Ebert relieved him of his office, but entrusted him with new duties. What remained was mutual respect, as Ebert wrote to Reinhardt in 1921: "It has been such a long hard road that this companionship will be a long, lasting tie." The close cooperation between Ebert and Reinhardt had started in the time of crisis during the revolution.

Noske's resignation heralded the end of the government of Chancellor Gustav Bauer (SPD). His successor would be Hermann Müller, leader of the Social Democratic Party. He stayed in office only until the Reichstag elections in June 1920. The trade unions, however, were not at all satisfied with the change of personnel. They continued the general strike even after the end of the Kapp-Lüttwitz Putsch, demanding fundamental reforms (even beyond the sphere of military policy) and influence in the formation of a new government. Ebert rejected their claims by pointing out that they were unconstitutional. Only the elected parliament had the constitutional right to adopt reforms; that remained the standard.

Friedrich Ebert still saw the extremist parties as a danger to the republic, as he stated in a letter to the Swedish prime minister, Hjalmar Branting, in April 1920:

> "Thus, we have to protect the democratic republic, for which we have fought for decades, not only against the Right but also against the Left. In fighting against military coup d'états and communist putsches we are fighting for the security of the republic. It cannot be ruled out that one day the putschists from both the Right and the Left will stand against us in one united front. [...] Above all, we must immediately remove the overtly reactionary officers from the army. This is not easy given the obvious lack of acceptable republican officers. Nevertheless, is has to be done. The same procedure has to be carried out in the administration. Here, too, suitable manpower is in short supply."

For new Minister of Defence Otto Gessler (DDP), the republic's preservation was not a chief concern. He declared himself a "rational republican" (*Vernunftrepublikaner*). He and General Hans von Seeckt, whom Ebert appointed as commander-in-chief of the army, kept the Reichswehr away from all party politics and vice versa. As a result, the Reichswehr was able to isolate itself from the republic and keep its political distance from the republican order. The president did not do enough to prevent this development.

In the wake of the putsch, Ebert intended to punish and discharge any anti-republicans still in uniform. Several officers had joined the conspirators, while others did not explicitly support the side of the legitimate and democratic government. Ebert persistently pressed for the expulsion of the putschists and their followers from the Reichswehr, however, nothing came of his insistence, because the Reichstag drew a line under the putsch by passing an amnesty bill. Only 172 officers were discharged, among them six generals. Not a single member of the Reichswehr was sent to prison for taking part in a putsch, and that was final.

Profound structural change and a more thoroughgoing democratic control of the military, as some Social Democrats constantly demanded, were not in accordance with Ebert's military policy. The final army law of March 1921 (*Wehrgesetz*) politically neutralised the military. Consequently, the Reichswehr did not become an integral part of democracy, but rather turned into a state within the state. It remained an alien element, and its leadership considered itself committed only to the abstract state and not necessarily as an institution dedicated to democracy. This development would have fatal implications for the future.

Until the Kapp-Lüttwitz Putsch, both the Reich president and the government had considered it self-evident to turn to the Reichswehr in order to maintain law and order. After the events in March 1920, the armed forces were relieved of this task. In March 1921, it was the *Preußische Schutzpolizei* (Prussian Armed State Police) that quelled the communist revolt in the industrial region of Central Germany, thus successfully going through its baptism by fire as keeper of the peace in crisis. In 1923, however, the military took over this function again.

The year 1923 brought in its wake the most severe crisis since the revolution, starting with the Franco-Belgian occupation of the Ruhr on 11 January. As a countermeasure, the German government called for "passive resistance", requesting that the population of the respective area withhold their cooperation from the occupiers. However, the refusal to work imposed and funded by the government caused astronomical inflation. Over the course of the economic and financial crises, the extremist elements on both the left and right fringes of the political spectrum boomed, such as the Communists on the left and the National Socialists and the various German nationalist groups on the right. Two further

On the border of the Ruhr valley, occupied by France since 1923: Ebert reaffirms the solidarity of the republic to the representatives of the occupied territory in Hamm in March 1923. He urges unity, stating the motto of the early labour movement: "All for one, and one for all."

conflicts developed which jeopardized national unity. Firstly, the disagreement between the Reich and the Bavarian government was coming to a head. Secondly, the Social Democrats in Central Germany entered government coalitions in Saxony and Thuringia with the anti-democratic KPD. Furthermore, the political Right was scheming for the establishment of a dictatorship. Over twelve months, no less than five coalition governments tried their luck at ruling. In the autumn of 1923, the fall of the Weimar Republic seemed imminent. As if by a miracle, however, the young state would survive.

This year of crisis started with the Cuno government, which proved to be incapable of coping with such a situation. For a long time, Ebert propped up "his" chancellor, who nevertheless resigned in the face of the growing opposition.

The formation of the "Grand Coalition" consisting of DVP, DDP, Centre Party, and SPD under Gustav Stresemann, leader of the right-liberal DVP, followed. Strongly supported by Ebert, this government was able to overcome the national existential crisis. First of all, the cabinet halted its policy of passive resistance in the Ruhr, which had financially ruined the country. Ebert backed the state-funded general strike until the bitter end, but ultimately, even he had to accept that they could no longer stay that course. Ending the passive resistance was the precondition for adjusting the currency, which was finally accomplished by introducing the so-called *Rentenmark*. As a result, inflation could be curbed and economic consolidation initiated. In order to master the crisis, the president was prepared to grant emergency decree powers to the new chancellor Stresemann in accordance with the controversial article 48 of the constitution, as he had done before with Cuno.

During his time in office, Ebert signed 136 regulations on the basis of article 48 of the constitution. Initially, the president used this capacity exclusively in order to restore general tranquillity, given his political belief in order. This course of action was in accordance with the Weimar Constitution. By using article 48 to justify emergency decrees in order to overcome a highly dramatic situation of economic and financial crisis, the constitution was stretched to the limits, representing a deeply questionable precedent in terms of constitutional law. Both the government and the president were convinced that they could only overcome the acute problems by using article 48. Ebert's course of action was guided by his concern to stabilise the jeopardised republic, while simultaneously always preserving and respecting the rights of the Reichstag. On the other hand, Paul von Hindenburg, his successor as head of state and former imperial field marshal general, was prepared to adeptly use the capabilities proscribed for him by article 48 in combination with further presidential powers against the Reichstag – that is to say against the republic. Preserving parliamentary rule was always Ebert's highest priority.

He had already professed his decisive resolve to protect the republic against its enemies in the speech he held after his election as Reich president before the National Assembly in February 1919:

> "Freedom and law are twins. Freedom can only take shape within a firm state order. Protecting and restoring this order wherever it has been violated has to be the highest priority for all who love freedom. We will fight tyranny, be it from the Left or from the Right, in any way we can."

However, Ebert's methods provoked objections, first and foremost in autumn 1923 – even from his own Social Democratic ranks. Most of the criticism was focused on the fact that Ebert had enabled Chancellor Stresemann in October to dismiss the Saxon government of Social Democrats and Communists, which had refused to give the Reich its allegiance. The Saxon KPD – a party in the state government – was gearing up for an open conflict with the republic. Stresemann intended to finally rectify the conflict with Saxony, which had been smouldering for months, and he adeptly pre-empted Social Democratic ministers in settlement of the matter. This process elicited bitter reproaches from Social Democrats meant not only for Stresemann but also for the president. An SPD member of the Reichstag said: "In my opinion Ebert is finished. How could he sign a regulation like that?"

To Ebert's disappointment, the Social Democrats, angry about the hasty and perhaps even avoidable course of action against Saxony, left the "Grand Coalition". Thus, Ebert's desired government coalition ended after just a few months. In his eyes, his party had made a drastic mistake in abandoning political power. This judgement proved correct. The SPD would spend the next five years in opposition. In Ebert's view, governing with a coalition, even if it necessitated compromising with a partner party, was always better than being completely left out from power as an opposition party. On the other hand, Ebert underestimated just under how much pressure the Social Democrats would be put were they to enter a coalition with the DVP, a party which intended to turn back the clock by reversing revolutionary achievements such as the eight-hour work day.

Social Democrats did not understand why nothing was done to hinder the anti-republican machinations conducted simultaneously by right-wing extremists in Bavaria. Although Ebert had demanded action in Munich, the leaders of the Reichswehr refused to give him their allegiance. Interventions did not take place until Adolf Hitler instigated a putsch in Munich on 9 November 1923 and ordered his followers to march on toward Berlin. The putsch was, however, thwarted.

At that time, Ebert appointed Hans von Seeckt, the commander-in-chief of the army, as the holder of executive authority, effectively granting him dictator-like powers. That was a risky move, as the general was flirting with a temporary dictatorship. However, Seeckt was unable to bring his plan to fruition, even after Chancellor Stresemann was forced to resign as a result of the passing of a vote of no-confidence in the Reichstag. The SPD supported the motion of no-confidence, although Ebert tried to prevent the chancellor's fall until the very end. Thus he admonished his party comrades: "The reason that led you to overthrow the chancellor will be forgotten in six weeks, but the consequences of your foolishness will still be felt ten years from now."

Thanks to the president, Stresemann's exit did not result in the dictatorship of General Seeckt, as sought by many. Despite the general's near unlimited power as the holder of executive authority, he depended on Ebert, who adroitly made Seeckt commit to the presidency, thus putting the would-be dictator in his place as soon as he threatened to exploit the government's position of weakness in order to expand his powers. In the conflicts between Seeckt and the ministers, Ebert always backed the new cabinet under Chancellor Wilhelm Marx (Centre Party). An open power struggle followed after Seeckt refused to comply with some of Ebert's requests. The president ultimately prevailed in this conflict.

On 13 February 1924, when the general called on Ebert to lift the state of emergency, his action was primarily born more out of resignation to the politicians' growing opposition rather than the belief that the time had come to return to political normalcy. The state of emergency had been an effective means to overcome the national crises and ultimately helped pave the way back into constitutional normality. Those responsible – first and foremost the president – had succeeded in curbing the extensive ambitions of the Reichswehr. Ebert had emerged the winner from the power struggle with Seeckt by effectively fending off the general's attempts of gaining more power. The Reichwehr's humbling proved one of the crucial preconditions for the process of relative internal stabilisation beginning in 1924. The republic overcame the crisis primarily thanks to the decisive action of the Reich president.

5 Representative of the Republic

Only by using each of his presidential powers did Friedrich Ebert succeed in saving the Reich as it stood on the brink of collapse. Over the course of these events, his alienation from his party reached its climax. Although the president and Social Democratic leadership always maintained contact, Ebert did not often take the opportunity to justify his policies in front of the Social Democratic committees and functionaries, or to ask for their understanding for his difficult situation when facing different constitutional issues. The Reich president was no longer a party politician; and he had not seen himself as such since February 1919. Ebert considered himself "the president for every German". The situation between him and the rest of the SPD did not improve after members of the Independent Social Democrats returned back to their original party, following the defection of their left wing to the KPD. Ebert had always wished for the reunification of the Social Democratic parties. However, when this became reality in autumn 1922, his personal relationship with the party leaders was affected. The SPD was changing. By then it was no longer the party of 1919, when Ebert had taken over the post of Reich president. His influence in the reunified SPD declined, consequently undermining his policy in support of a grand coalition. In June 1923, Ebert wrote to a party friend that the reunification of the SPD "weighed heavily on the party's shoulders". This was also an accurate description of his feeling of unease caused by the consequences of the Social Democrats' reunification after their split in 1917.

Over the course of time, the strain with his own party increased. From the moment the SPD left the Grand Coalition in autumn 1923, differences almost inevitably emerged as a result of the constitutional position of the Reich president and Ebert's understanding that the office should be executed in a nonpartisan manner. At the party convention in 1924, some members of lower party organisations made a motion to exclude the former party leader, Friedrich Ebert, from their ranks because he had agreed to impose the central government's Executive Order (*Reichsexekution*) on Saxony and the Saxon state government. The SPD leadership wholeheartedly backed Ebert by not even allowing the motion of no-confidence to be put to the vote. However, this event could not hide the friction between the president and the

Social Democratic Party. The saddler union, on the other hand, expelled Ebert after decades of membership.

That certainly hit Ebert very hard. In contrast to the differences between him and his party – differences he bemoaned time and again and which affected him personally – the bourgeois parties met him with growing respect. Ebert's manner of executing his office was "promotion for the republic", as the novelist Thomas Mann, the later Nobel laureate, astutely put it in October 1922:

> "Ebert, for instance, I know. A fundamentally sympathetic man possessing both dignity and modesty and not lacking in humour; temperate, human, steadfast. I have seen him a few times performing with friendliness and poise the duties of his office at ceremonies; he was, in his ceremonial black coat, the picture of a favourite of fortune, talented, a citizen among citizens [...]. And I have got the impression, which I invite you to share with me, that it is possible for democracy to be more German than imperial grand opera."

It is safe to assume that the great German novelist was representative of the bourgeois and democratic camp in its appreciation of the Social Democratic Reich president. A relationship of mutual respect and recognition developed between the republic's poet laureate, Gerhart Hauptmann, winner of the Nobel Prize for literature in 1912, and the Reich president. Both appreciated one another. Ebert had earned this respect for his nonpartisan administration and for his efforts to overcome political barriers. This was true for many, yet by no means for everyone in the bourgeois milieu.

Conservatives and monarchists, on the other hand, saw him as nothing more than a saddler who had lost his way and mistakenly ended up on the throne. They cultivated their snobbery towards the craftsman who had gained the highest public office, a representative of Social Democracy ostracised during the Kaiserreich. Leftist intellectuals such as Kurt Tucholsky, however, sarcastically criticised Ebert as a bureaucrat and a bloodless paper pusher ("*Papiermensch*"). According to the left-wing author Maximilian Harden, "Friderico Ebert" was a pathetic bourgeois ("*armseliger Spießbürger*"), a revolutionary in word only ("*Mundrevolutionär*") and "*Überpatriot*", the undereducated Reich saddler ("*Reichssattler*") of insufficient intellectual calibre, a "Social Democrat of mediocrity", a "tailor's son, journeyman saddler, publican, tab publisher, party secretary, party cashier", incapable and unworthy of wielding the highest public office. These brilliantly-phrased poisoned arrows aimed at the head of state, but they also hit the republic and did a disservice to the young Weimar democracy by damaging its reputation. Georg Grosz, the well-known artist with close ties to the Communist party, portrayed Friedrich Ebert the way the radical left saw the Reich president, a mere lackey of the industrial magnate Hugo Stinnes. Grosz depicted Ebert as a "labour traitor" and an instrument of the big industry, an image commonly held by the Communists since the political changes of November 1918.

However, the Reich president was undeterred by such accusations and criticism, and continued to promote democracy. His notion of society was based on the idea of a national community. His understanding of that national community, however, was by no means similar to the authoritarian, excluding, and distorted sense of "*Volksgemeinschaft*" later propagated by the National Socialists. In stark contrast to National Socialism's notion of national race, Friedrich Ebert's concept of a people's community, which he repeatedly advocated, was based on political equality, freedom, and unity. In October 1922, he wrote that he intended to "balance differences and to strengthen the feeling of togetherness of all the social strata of our fatherland". In 1919, he had warned in his Easter letter to the National Assembly: "Bring your-

Friedrich Ebert and Gerhart Hauptmann.

selves to stop being self-destructive." Such appeals were typical of Ebert during his entire time in office.

Ebert was again following his maxim of unity by working towards a harmonic cooperation between the Reich and the individual states. In the weeks after the November revolution, Ebert did his utmost to avoid any discussion of the reorganisation of the individual German states of various sizes. First and foremost, the liquidation and reorganisation of multiple smaller constituent states (*Kleinstaaten*) and breaking Prussia's oppressive dominance within the Reich were under consideration, but not by Ebert. He was not prepared to grasp the nettle, and thus the territorial issue remained unsolved. Nevertheless, he included the constituent states in the debate on reorganisation.

Over the course of the transition from the Kaiserreich to the Republic of Weimar, Ebert changed from a centralist into a rational federalist. During the proceedings of the revolutionary government on the drafting of the constitution on 14 January 1919, Ebert's fellow Social Democratic people's deputy, Otto Landsberg, emphatically championed the centralised state. Ebert replied to him that maintaining the unity of the Reich was only possible on a federal basis, given the predictable opposition of the Southern states to a centralised state. When the original draft of the constitution, written by the liberal and state secretary of the interior Hugo Preuß, was met with criticism from the representatives of the individual states due to its centralist tendencies, Ebert poured oil on troubled waters by assuring them "that a united Reich is possible only on the foundation of a federal state", and that the central government did not have the slightest intention "of violating the federal states". Ebert did, however, warn against exaggerating their states' rights. At the opening of the National Assembly on 6 February 1919, he denounced excessive emphasis on the specific interests of the individual states. Germany should not fall victim to "the misery of fragmentation and restriction once again".

Even as head of state, Ebert always saw himself as the advocate of the individual states. He travelled south on his first trip through Germany in August and September 1919. That made sense for two key reasons. For one thing, because according to the new Reich constitution, Bavaria, Württemberg, and Saxony would lose their autonomous military contingents, all of which were to be incorporated into the future Reichswehr. Furthermore, reservations to a centralised government in Berlin were strongest in the South, where fervent federalists, who saw their states forced into a centralised corset of sorts by the new republic, were at home. Thus, Ebert faced glaring criticism for the recently adopted constitution on his first tour as Reich president. He asked for understanding in view of Germany's current catastrophic situation resulting from the war, which necessitated the transfer of several rights traditionally exercised by the individual states to the authority of the Reich:

> "Maintaining the German tribes' identities and the independent political life of the single states, unifying the Reich and protecting the characteristics of those German tribes are certainly compatible."

These words, which were phrased in a contemporary manner of speaking, mentioning "tribes" and "tribe characteristics", showed considerable understanding for the worries of the individual states. Although he stressed time and again that he was a "South German with all his heart" and sympathised with his headstrong fellow southerners, his visit was by no means easy. It was not a rhetorical balancing act when Ebert emphasised the independent political life of the single states and the necessity to strengthen the Reich at the same time. According to him, the new republic had to avoid any "damaging particularism at the expense of the greater whole".

"Diversity within unity", that was his message. Already by his first trip, Ebert, contrary to what was to be expected from a Social Democrat working in Berlin, did not come across as the representative of a centralist state. He rather presented himself as a head of state striving for compromise, reassuring the individual states that the government of the Reich had no intention of depriving them of their regional cultural identity or their political sovereignty.

The head of state with a group of children in Berlin in celebration of the reception of a group of American children's aid representatives in the gardens of the Presidential Palace, June 1924.

On his first trip through the southern states – which was not followed by a second, longer tour of the rest of Germany – Ebert acted noticeably reserved at his public appearances. It seems as though he underestimated both the power of public representation and the chance offered by active public relations. In terms of symbolic politics, the republican head of state could not just follow in the footsteps of the last Hohenzollern. Ebert neither wished to, nor could afford to be a cheap imitation of the Kaiser. The sabre-rattling appearances of Emperor Wilhelm II could not serve as an example for the democratic head of state. Ebert's style of representation lacked the pomp and circumstance of his predecessor, still considered standard practice by the public of the former German Empire.

By avoiding any cult of personality, Ebert tried to embed the concept of the republic into public awareness. He was a reserved representative of the new state order. Ebert's public persona as president did not mirror his personality when among friends, around whom he could be impulsive, humorous, and sarcastic. The President Friedrich Ebert was no longer the powerfully eloquent Social Democratic functionary from pre-war times who was able to cast a spell on his supporters, indeed owing his career within the labour movement to his talent as a public speaker. As president, however, he came across as a dry and overly functional head of state, a stern and sober statesman. He held his office without pretence and pathos, without the opportunistic use of bombastic speeches or symbolic yet emotionally powerful acts.

Ebert was no well-known royal regent in uniform, whom his subjects would meet in person at least once in their lifetime. He represented the ever-increasingly bourgeois and dull republic, which was unable to reach the hearts of the people. Awakening enthusiasm, appearing as a man of the people and mingling with the crowd was not in his nature and far from his concept of politics. Ebert lacked aura. Over the course of time, he made public appearances with declining tendency rather more seldom than often. His reserved and austere representation shaped the public image of the new head of state.

The citizens of the Weimar Republic did not see their head of state very often in person. Very much in the same unobtrusive manner, and almost incomprehensibly, Ebert did not use any other means of public relations. He did not have a personal photographer or correspondent to cannily portray him in order to popularise his persona. Not enough was done to shape the image of the president among the public through photographs and articles. Illustrated magazines primarily published official staged half- and full-body portraits of the president, though never appearing casually dressed and in down-to-earth manner.

Ebert was not the type of politician who wished to constantly be present in the mass media. He and his small staff

Friedrich Ebert (second from the right) with the Minister of Defense Gustav Noske (third from the right) and acquaintances swimming in the Baltic Sea in 1919. Ebert would carry the photograph with him until the end of his days. Opponents of democracy in Germany used the photography in order to disparage Ebert personally as well as the republic.

of advisors in the presidential palace did not seize the opportunity offered by the intensive use of mass media to help increase the popularity of the head of state. Thus, there are hardly any film recordings of him other than a mere few sequences of a couple minutes duration each. That is all. It was only late – too late and even then too cautious – when Ebert and his staff finally started a public relations campaign, which explains why the infamous photograph that showed Ebert and his minister of defence, Gustav Noske, wading in the Baltic Sea in swimming trunks could become such a sensational and at the same time questionable "success". The private shot was published in the "*Berliner Illustrierte Zeitung*", the most widely read illustrated magazine in Germany, on 21 August 1919, just when the president was sworn into office according to the new constitution of the republic. The picture had enormous impact. The public, only used to the pomp of Imperial Germany, responded to the photograph with unexpected shock. The author Joseph Roth rightly pointed out in 1923 that the photograph became the "most forceful argument against the republic because of also being the most plebeian". Anti-republicans from right to left published the picture in several variations and in a plethora of caricatures without these attacks being answered effectively enough in the media.

Regardless the unobtrusive representation, the head of state often took the initiative to create awareness among the entire German people for the republic, to promote identification with the new democracy, and to build up an intellectual foundation based on democratic traditions. Ebert's goal became finding points of reference to German history to use as a compass, and creating symbols with which both the different social strata and the political parties could identify. Already at the opening of the National Assembly, Ebert had referred to the "spirit of Weimar", the spirit of great poets such as Goethe and Schiller, as an example for the republic, even bringing together the traditions of the revolutions from 1848 and 1918:

> "Here in Weimar, we have to accomplish the transition from imperialism to idealism, from a world power to an intellectual giant [...]. Now, the spirit of Weimar, the spirit of our great philosophers and poets, has to impregnate us once again."

Ebert firmly supported the celebrations of the 75th anniversary of the first German parliament of 1848 (*Paulskirchenversammlung*), which took place in Frankfurt in 1923. On the Römerberg in the Hessian city, where tens of thousands met and celebrated the republic, Ebert experienced the kind of society of free citizens living in harmony and across classes, the republican people's community he had heralded time and again, the unity in the service of democracy – this event created a feeling of elation which was rare on his trips and public appearances.

On Constitution Day 1922, Ebert proclaimed the "Song of the Germans" (*Das Lied der Deutschen*), written in 1841 by Hoffmann von Fallersleben, as Germany's national anthem. He particularly emphasised the third verse because of its chorus of "unity and justice and freedom". A discussion emerged in the following years (and again after 1945) as to whether this verse alone should become the national anthem (as it is today). In addition to that, Ebert supported the idea of instituting a public holiday to honour the constitution on 11 August, the day it was signed by Ebert in his Thuringian holiday resort town Schwarzburg, south of Weimar, in 1919. On this day, republicans should show their colours. However, given the diversity within German society, which was separated into many cultural and social groups, many of which opposed the republic, this did not develop the intended integrative appeal. Constitution Day, as the substitute of a national founding day, never became a popular public holiday which attracted all classes and sectors of society. Many preferred to stay away from the event and thus to openly show their distance to the republic. Democracy was not the ideal political system of government for all Germans.

6 Victim of Defamation

By using these symbolic acts, the Reich president intended to create values of tradition which would promote the new political order. One can safely assume that Ebert succeeded in winning over the politically undecided people to democracy. He did not, however, reach the Communists, who dreamed of the world revolution and worked towards the dictatorship of the proletariat. Anti-republican monarchists, who held firm and unshakable resentment towards the new democracy, were also immune to Ebert's persuasion. For them, the republic was nothing else than the despicable system of the "November criminals" and a creation of the former enemies of the Reich. As head of state, Ebert, who was more a representative of the republic than any other politician, came into the line of fire of the anti-democrats. The radical left pegged him as traitor to the workers because he had opposed the establishment of a Soviet-styled republic and had allegedly formed an alliance with the old elites during the revolution in order to suppress the labour movement. The radical right, on the other hand, in their blind hatred of the republic, initiated an incredible defamatory campaign against the Reich president.

Slandering the head of state became socially acceptable. Political culture took a turn towards the increasingly vulgar. The radical press made outrageous allegations against Ebert. The anti-democrats poured scorn on him in words and pictures referring to his trajectory from the Pfaffengasse in Heidelberg to the Wilhelmstraße in Berlin (the government district in the capital city), from itinerant journeyman saddler and publican in Bremen to president of the Reich. Rumours of corruption, personal enrichment, alcoholism, and immoral conduct circulated. The defamatory campaign did not even spare his wife Louise, who also fell victim to slander.

In the beginning, Ebert did not take much notice of these assaults. After former Minister of Finance Matthias Erzberger (1921) and Foreign Minister Walther Rathenau (1922) were murdered by right-wing extremists, he began to press charges against the authors of the insults more frequently. Following Rathenau's murder, he wrote to Gerhart Hauptmann:

> "I look upon this deplorable act with deep concern […] it is a bitter realisation that such iniquities return us to the thorny and rocky path which quiet reflection and clear insight of the achievable have indicated us to be the sole feasible option […]. Nevertheless, we must decidedly persevere beyond it, and work toward the recovery and renewal of our people."

Turning to the law became a means for him in the struggle against the enemies of the republic. He initiated over 200 trials. However, libel suits proved to be a blunt instrument in the fight for the reputation of the republic and against the systematic witch hunt.

By accusing Ebert of treason – the most offensive allegation –, the anti-democrats continued their "stab-in-the-back myth" (*Dolchstoßlegende*), which permanently poisoned the political atmosphere of the Weimar Republic. They blamed the organised labour movement of having stabbed Germany's valiant troops in the back, and having caused Germany's defeat with their revolutionary actions at the home front. Reactionary monarchists, who despised the republic, were more than happy to instrumentalise these accusations. Through those means, the political and military leaders of the Kaiserreich could be exonerated of any responsibility in Germany's defeat and its consequences, first and foremost the Treaty of Versailles, which was regarded as a national humiliation. It was a welcome opportunity to pillory the Reich president as a traitor in order to blame the new republican politicians for Germany's woes. The defamatory accusations hinted at the workers' strike in Berlin from January 1918. At that time, when hundreds of thousands of ammunition workers laid down their tools, the Social Democratic leader Friedrich Ebert joined the strike committee with the intention of ending the industrial dispute without damage to the Reich and without negative consequences for the workers, though due to the adamant attitude of the Imperial Reich government he did not succeed. The strike also played an important role during his time as president. The most spectacular treason trial staged by the anti-democrats in their campaign against the republic took place in Magdeburg. It ended in a scandal on 23 December 1924. The judge came to the conclusion that the strike of January 1918 indeed constituted an act of treason, and thus officially declared Ebert a traitor to his country. Ebert was deeply offended. From that point on, every sceptic of democracy, from white collar intellectual to working class citizen at the pub desk, could brand the republican head of state as "traitor" and go unpunished. Ebert was not about to take this allegation lying down. He pressed for an appeal to overturn the judgement at first instance because it discredited the entire republic by causing an odour of illegitimacy born out of betrayal. On 24 December 1924, he wrote to the DVP politician Katharina von Oheimb:

> "I will face further course of the proceedings with a clear conscience. Personally, I do not need a legal verdict against defamatory attacks; it is only in the interest of the state that I saw myself compelled to take steps. However, state interest and judicature seem to be almost incompatible at present."

Besides his disappointment, Ebert also expresses moments of confidence in his letter from the Christmas Eve of 1924 to Oheimb, "my path in life was never strewn with roses. I do not wish anything else for the future. Nevertheless, I will further follow my own path, confident and firm, in good spirits and with a clear conscience!" His path would, however, not be much longer. Until the trial in Magdeburg, it had been taken for granted that Friedrich Ebert would run for office in the presidential elections of spring 1925, all the more since his party had made peace with him over the course of the defamatory campaign and nominated him as the Social Democratic candidate. Ebert even informed himself as to how the contemporary American president had organised his campaign, and sought to apply that strategy in the coming German election. The verdict of Magdeburg, however, made him change his mind. After several stressful years of political work he rather preferred to retire into private life and move back to Heidelberg.

His home town of Heidelberg always held a special place in his heart. Whenever he was on an official trip in the South of Germany, he visited it. He often spent his holidays in Freudenstadt in the Black Forest. Between 1921 and 1924, he spent several weeks in the spa-town Bad Mergentheim in Württemberg to relieve the bilious complaint he had been suffering from as early as during the war. In 1916 he had had a breakdown after giving a speech. He could only just avoid an operation.

In June 1922 he had to interrupt his holiday in Freudenstadt after receiving the news about the assassination of Foreign Minister Rathenau. That same night, Ebert suffered a severe bilious attack. Contrary to medical advice, he travelled by train to Berlin after being given morphine injections in order to deliver the memorial address – in spite of intense pain – for the murdered minister. He suffered another attack on Whitsun of 1924 during a short recovery stay in the Schorfheide, north of Berlin, where he often retired for respite from everyday political life to a remote hunter's cabin near Lake Werbellin, where he used to hunt. However, these were only very brief periods of an otherwise exhausting and stressful life.

His dream of a peaceful retirement in his home town of Heidelberg did not come true. Ebert indirectly fell victim to the defamatory campaign. After the judgement of Magdeburg he complained often about health problems. His general practitioner had originally diagnosed him with bilious colics, instead of appendicitis, which was the actual reason for his pain. Ebert failed to act upon medical advice of relaxing in a spa, because he wanted to be over and done with the appeal to the Magdeburg decision. On 23 February, his health condition worsened dramatically. That same night he had to undergo surgery in a Berlin clinic – too late, as it turned out. On 28 February 1925 at about 10:15 am, Friedrich Ebert succumbed to complications brought on by appendicitis and

Memorial service for the deceased president in Berlin. More than a million people fill the streets.

the belated surgery. There is no doubt that the defamatory campaign contributed to his early death at the age of 54. According to his practitioner's record, the "emotional agitation" caused by the Magdeburg trial had weakened the patient's resilience to such an extent that he did not survive surgery.

Berlin bid farewell to Ebert at a moving republican memorial ceremony on 4 March. An enormous crowd – an estimated one million people – accompanied the funeral procession. The next day Ebert was laid to rest in the central cemetery in Heidelberg (*Bergfriedhof*). This was the end of a politician whose life's aim had been the implementation of Social Democracy. During the revolution, the Social Democrat and reform politician Friedrich Ebert had paved the way for the republic, always prioritising the democratic parliamentary system. As head of state of the republic, he saw himself as president of all Germans instead of as a representative of one party. Based on this understanding of the office, it was his main objective to keep democracy in good working order. In this, he was not completely unsuccessful.

Two weeks before his death, the "*Vorwärts*", the official newspaper of the SPD, had reminded its readers of the sixth anniversary of Ebert's election as Reich president. According to the newspaper, "comrade Ebert" had been forced in a time of crisis to shoulder a task more difficult than anything that any other accountable statesman before him had been confronted with. The periodical described the challenges Ebert encountered as Reich president in the following way:

> "Hardest pressure from without, deepest shock within, social hardship, looming disintegration – these were the circumstances when Ebert took office. After that the decision on Upper Silesia, the London ultimatum, the Ruhr struggle, then coups from the left, coups from the right, political murderers, separatism in the West and in Bavaria, finally hunger riots and inflation."

As brief as it is, the analysis of initial circumstances and hardships during Ebert's time in office could not have been more precise. The party showed respect for the achievements of its former leader as the head of the republic: "It was Ebert's task to prevent crises from turning into disasters." Indeed, crises had not developed into disasters. In 1925, the year when the first Reich president died, the Weimar Republic was enjoying a time of relative stability – not least thanks to the policies of Friedrich Ebert – after years of severe crisis and controversy. Friedrich Ebert had done what a head of state, decisively and determinedly committed to the democratic ideal, could do given the republic's segmented and domestically imbalanced society, which had hardly been pacified, and suffered under significant foreign pressure from without. When Ebert died, the Weimar Republic lost one of

Friedrich Ebert's grave in the Bergfriedhof (Central Cemetery) in Heidelberg.

its pioneers and pillars. The inscription on his gravestone summarises the political guideline which he had chosen as his chief principle in 1919: "The purpose of my work is the welfare of the people" ("*Des Volkes Wohl ist meiner Arbeit Ziel*"). This was an epitaph befitting the philosophy that the Reich president managed to implement in spite of manifold obstacles, thus making Ebert, the Social Democrat and republican statesman, a precursor of modern German democracy. The republic would soon realise what a loss it had suffered with the death of the first Reich president.

V Friedrich Ebert in Political Memory and in Historical Research

In June 1924, the Social Democratic chairman Hermann Müller defended the Reich president against his critics from within the party at its convention:

> "It goes without saying that we as a party do not accept everything for which the Reich president has to take responsibility [...] If there will be a historian in the future trying to objectively assess the era of Ebert as head of the German Republic, then he will find out the extent of insight and discretion with which Ebert had held his office. The Social Democratic Party will be eternally honoured to have had a man in its own ranks who under extremely difficult circumstances had an impact as great as Ebert had."

The first Reich president died less than a year later. Friedrich Ebert's untimely and – in the eyes of his contemporaries – tragic death has shaped his image until deep into the time of the German Federal Republic. In a speech given in 1950, Theodor Heuss, the first president of the Federal Republic, called Ebert the "Abraham Lincoln of German history". This comparison soon became a well-known saying. Heuss had first used it in his obituary for Ebert in 1925, but it was the British newspaper "*The Observer*" which coined the expression in autumn 1923 when it compared Ebert's attempts to maintain the Reich with the efforts of the American president to preserve the union of the United States during the American Civil War (1861–1865). Heuss wrote in 1927, "future histories will someday recognise Ebert's service [...] that he guided Germany out of revolutionary fomentation and chaos,

The president with his wife walking through the streets of Berlin to place his vote in the parliamentary elections of June 1920.

and set it on the course of democracy". It would, however, take a long time until this judgment was universally accepted.

Social Democrats and their commemoration of the Weimar Republic turned the first Reich president into a symbol of the new democratic order in stark contrast to his successor Paul von Hindenburg, the former imperial field marshal. Immediately after Ebert's death, the "*Friedrich-Ebert-Stiftung*" was founded to support students from working-class families. However, Ebert never became a political legend outside of his party. After their seizure of power in 1933, the Nazis tried to wipe out the memory of Ebert, whom they maligned as a "November criminal". Yet his name lived on in resistance groups and among exiled Germans. After the Second World War, Ebert's memory increasingly gained political and historical awareness, but without achieving broader recognition.

Apart from only a few bibliographical attempts, historians and scholarly research widely ignored Friedrich Ebert. It was not until the 100th anniversary of his birth in 1971, that an account of Ebert's life and works based on substantial source material was published for the first time by Peter-Christian Witt, who modestly advertised it as a biographical essay. Despite some further publications, Ebert, nonetheless, never became the subject of any extensive academic biography.

That was partly due to Ebert's non-existent estate and partly due to his personality. He did not display a bombastic or ostentatious attitude characterised by breaks and changes of his career unlike some of his contemporaries such as Gustav Stresemann or Walther Rathenau, both of whom have enjoyed the interest of historical researchers. There was never a fundamental change in Ebert's political philosophy. He did not have the charisma of a great politician, which usually intrigues historians in influential historical figures. In addition to his personality, which hardly tempted any historical research, it has not been beneficial that there are few surviving primary sources (written by Ebert himself). During his time as Reich president, Ebert destroyed most his documents himself. The rest burned during an air raid in 1943 when his widow's flat in Berlin was destroyed. Thus, to this very day, Ebert is mostly remembered for his time as a politician during the revolutionary time period rather than as Reich president. Long-nurtured stereotypes of his attitude during that time still dominate the historical memory of the politician and statesman.

Beyond historical research, he was seen as the one who paved the way to democracy during the revolution and who prevented Germany from being "bolshevised" and turned into a Soviet-like dictatorship similar to Russia's after the First World War. Assessments like these confirmed the existing historiography of the post war period which were predominantly conservative, and which esteemed, and even idealised, Ebert in every respect. This interpretation found its expression in German history books and in West German school books until well into the 1980s.

In the Eastern German Democratic Republic (*Deutsche Demokratische Republik*; GDR) Ebert was disparaged as a "traitor to the labour movement", because of his struggle against the establishment of a Soviet republic, for his belief in parliamentary democracy, and his alleged cooperation with the old elites of the Kaiserreich, which was consistent with the traditional condemnation by Communists in his lifetime. That remained a constant, even though its presentation varied in intensity. The first president's son Friedrich Ebert Jr. was a senior member of the SED (*Sozialistische Einheitspartei Deutschlands*: the single party dictatorship in the GDR) and long-term mayor of East-Berlin (GDR), and endorsed the critical assessment of the role his father played, particularly in 1918/19. However, he strongly rejected the verdict that his father had been a "traitor to the labour movement".

Whereas Ebert's descendants in East Germany did not have the opportunity to counter the assessment of Ebert which prevailed in the GDR, his surviving relatives – his widow Louise and his son Karl, who would spend the rest of their days in Heidelberg – did not make any effort to shape or influence Ebert's image. In the German Federal Republic, the appraisal of Ebert changed over the course of intensive research on the revolutionary period. Predominantly left-wing Social Democratic historical work in the 1960s concluded that the majority of the workers' and soldiers' councils had had a Social Democratic orientation, and that they supported Ebert's policy towards parliamentary democracy in contrast to the former scholarly assertions that they had been radical or communist. A transformation similar to that of Russia was not on the councils' agenda from 1918 to 1919; it was not about the alternative between democracy and a dictatorship along Soviet lines. According to this perspective, Ebert's policy appeared in a completely different light. He lost his halo as the saviour of German democracy from Bolshevism.

However, this new scholarly research, which investigated the causes of the republic's end in 1933, discovered the revolutionary government's failures when the foundations of democracy were laid. According to this view, the Social Democrats, and their figurehead Ebert in particular, squandered the opportunity to implement structural measures that might have secured parliamentary democracy between 9 November 1918 and 6 February 1919 (the day of the inauguration of the National Assembly), the period of time today most commonly referred to as the "open period". It has been asserted that Ebert clung to the concept of order *ad absurdum*, and that he lacked the political imagination and the clear perspective necessary in times of revolution.

The underlying thesis of this line of historiography is that, during the period of transition, too few reforms that might have provided a solid foundation for the first German democracy were realised. The cooperation with the old elites in administrative and military matters was far closer than required, and structural reforms regarded as necessary were not even initiated. This view, which highlights the reproach of "missed opportunities" – and occasionally idealises the revolutionary movement as an example of grassroots democracy – claims that the workers' and soldiers' councils were indeed an influential power, and therefore Ebert and the revolutionary government negligently squandered an opportunity to renew the political, economic, and social system. This new interpretation reaches far, however, as the latest research and its hypothesis fail to address some core questions. How should this potential, which was by no means democratically legitimised, have been put to use? Was it indeed vital for the survival of the republic to introduce reforms such as the socialisation of major industries? And finally, would a systematic reform policy have effectively stabilised the republic during the revolutionary period? There is good reason to assume that a counter-revolution would have throttled the new democracy at birth in the case of fundamental economic and social intervention. Much of this discourse is counterproductive. In general, the hypothetical question of "what if?" cannot be answered.

Apart from many speculative deductions, critics from far beyond historical research viewed the failure to institute such structural reform on the part of Ebert and the People's Deputies as a crucial mistake, which not only damaged the republic but was also responsible for its transition into dictatorship in January 1933. Such an approach, however, underestimates the preconditions in the revolutionary period and the narrow time frame. Furthermore, it completely ignores Ebert's basic democratic principle of offering all citizens the right to political participation as well as his greater political vision: the parliamentary republic. That was his main objective, and the fact that he was able to achieve this goal at all given the deso-

The Pfaffengasse in Heidelberg in the early 1920's, where Ebert is born in 1871.

late circumstances of 9 November 1918 was quite an accomplishment.

Despite different assessments of Ebert's politics during the revolution, there has been no *Historikerstreit* or intellectual disagreement concerning the legacy of Friedrich Ebert, as the Social Democratic weekly newspaper "*Vorwärts*" saw it in the weeks leading up the 70th anniversary of his election as Reich president. Ebert and his political achievements are hardly the right source for a scholarly "dispute", even though there is no unanimous assessment of the Reich president Ebert, who only vaguely appears in the judgment of historical accounts of the Weimar Republic.

In general, studies concerning the revolutionary period adequately factor in Ebert's politics and political strategies during this time, even though they do not reach the same conclusion. There has also been sufficient biographical research of Ebert's life prior to 1918/19 when he became chancellor and People's Deputy. Ebert as Reich president, however, has been widely ignored by historical research. As a result, Ebert has been reduced to a symbol of Weimar Social Democracy, struggling, and ultimately failing, to completely cope with the challenges presented by transition. Historical publications occasionally characterised Ebert as an example of a petty-minded, unimaginative, Social Democratic representative of the petit bourgeois in a government office. There are some blatantly coined phrases attempting to portray Ebert in such a light which resurfaced time again: "A German Lincoln or a Stalin of the SPD?" headlined "*Die Zeit*", a German weekly, in 1975 on occasion of the 50th anniversary of Ebert's death. These characterisations were as catchy as they were erroneous. Comparisons with other historical figures merely served the purpose of creating an easily remembered phrase in order to portray – and indeed typecast – Ebert.

No noteworthy scholarly study on Ebert as Reich president existed until 2006 when an extensive biographic account was published for the first time. The biography was based on sources from different and widespread backgrounds and focused on his years as head of state. It has debunked many long accepted myths (*Walter Mühlhausen: Friedrich Ebert*

1871–1925. Reichspräsident der Weimarer Republik, Bonn. sec. ed. 2007). The assessment of Ebert and his policies also took current political changes into consideration. Over the course of the German reunification of 1990, several difficulties became apparent as being persistent and long-lasting, highlighting the even more challenging problems after the First World War with all their consequences: the time constraints on the decisions taken during the revolution in 1918/19, and the first fragile years of the republic absent any economic and political success necessary for the acceptance of the new order – a success the Federal Republic was lucky enough to produce after the Second World War. Apart from the merely biographical approach, a greater consideration was given to the scope of action of the Majority Social Democrats under Ebert in order to characterise the time of the Weimar Republic. As a result, the People's Deputy and the first Reich president appeared in a much more positive light. This view stresses that it had been possible to lay the foundation for a parliamentary democracy despite the disastrous situation at the end of the war. It emphasises that there was, in fact, a real chance for the republic to develop into a solid democracy by the end of Ebert's time in office as president. In short, the downfall of the republic in 1933 was not the inevitable result of 1918/19.

Shortly before the collapse of the German Democratic Republic, the exhibition in the *Reichspräsident-Friedrich-Ebert-Gedenkstätte* (Reich President Friedrich Ebert Memorial) in Heidelberg celebrated its opening. The beginnings of the memorial can be seen as far back as the 1960's. In May 1962, the Friedrich Ebert-Foundation and the city of Heidelberg initiated an exhibition in the house where Ebert was born. In 1982, efforts were made to expand this exhibition into a national memorial. Thus, it appeared as though Ebert did not rank among the more widely-known historical figures. The German *Bundestag* passed the bill to establish the Reich

President Friedrich Ebert Memorial Foundation against the votes of the members of the Green Party in December 1986. The mission statement of the foundation is "to preserve the memory of the first German Reich president, Friedrich Ebert, and to contribute to the understanding of the German history of his era". The memorial site was opened on 11 February 1989, the 70th anniversary of Ebert's election as president. With the establishment of this foundation, the Federal Republic officially and institutionally honoured the merits and memory of Friedrich Ebert.

The birthplace of Friedrich Ebert – today the entrance to the Memorial in the Pfaffengasse.

The core of the memorial in Heidelberg is the small flat where Ebert was born in 1871 as the son of a tailor. Here are the roots of the great Social Democrat and statesman, the founder and guarantor of the first German democracy, who has finally found his rightful place within the historical and political tradition of the Federal Republic of Germany.

Timeline

18 January 1871	Proclamation of Wilhelm I of Prussia as German Emperor in Versailles, France
4 February 1871	Birth of Friedrich Ebert in Heidelberg, the seventh of nine children to Karl Ebert (1834–1892), a tailor, and Katharina Ebert, née Hinkel (1834–1897)
19 March 1871	Baptism of Ebert into the Roman Catholic faith
22–27 May 1875	Merger of the General German Workers' Association (*Allgemeiner Deutscher Arbeiterverein*) and the Social Democratic Workers' Party (*Sozialdemokratische Arbeiterpartei*) under the name Socialist Workers' Party of Germany (*Sozialistische Arbeiterpartei Deutschlands*)
1877–1885	Ebert's elementary school years
21 October 1878	Promulgation of first Anti-Socialist Law by the Reichstag at the request of Imperial Chancellor Otto von Bismarck in order to suppress Social Democracy, constantly renewed until 1890
1885–1888	Ebert's apprenticeship as saddler
1888–1918	Reign of Emperor Wilhelm II
1889–1891	Ebert's travels with stops in Hanover, Kassel, Wesel, Quakenbrück among others
1889	Ebert joins the Social Democratic Party and the trade union of saddlers
May 1891	Arrival in Bremen. Employment as saddler
12–18 October 1890	First party conference of the Social Democrats after the passing of the Anti-Socialist Laws, new name for the party: Social Democratic Party of Germany
14–18 October 1891	SPD conference in Erfurt; adoption of the "Erfurt Programme"
1893/94	Ebert works as editor of the Social Democratic "*Bremer-Bürger-Zeitung*"
2 March 1894	Elected as chairman of the Social Democratic Association in Bremen (until 1896)
13 April 1984	Ebert takes over an inn, publican until 1900
9 May 1894	Marriage to working-class woman Louise Rump (23 December 1873–18 January 1955); children: Friedrich (1894–1979), Georg (1896–1917), Heinrich

	(1897–1917), Karl (1899–1975), and Amalie (1900–1931)
11–16 October 1896	Ebert first attends an SPD party congress in Gotha
15 December 1899	Election as a member of the *Bremer Bürgerschaft* (state parliament of Bremen), serving until 1905. Selection as leader of the parliamentary group of the SPD
19 December 1899	Ebert's election as workers' secretary of the trade unions, serving until 1905
14–20 August 1904	Attendance at the International Congress of Socialists in Amsterdam
18–24 September 1904	Ebert's selection as one of two leaders of the SPD party conference in Bremen
24 September 1905	Election as secretary of the SPD party executive, winning 174 out of 283 votes at the party congress in Jena
1 December 1905	Move to Berlin
1905–1913	Membership in the SPD executive
December 1908	Chairman of the Central Office for the Working Youth of Germany
28 August – 3 September 1910	Attendance at the International Congress of Socialists in Copenhagen
16 September 1911	Election of Hugo Haase as Chairman of the SPD. Ebert's reception of 102 out of 393 votes cast of in spite of renouncing his candidacy for the position
25 January 1912	Election of Ebert as member of the Reichstag, representing Elberfeld-Barmen (Wuppertal)
1912–1918	Member of the Reichstag
20 September 1913	Ebert's Election as one of two party leaders, wining with 433 out of 473 votes at the SPD party convention in Jena
1913–1919	Ebert's tenure as one of two SPD chairmen
1/3 August 1914	Declaration of war by Germany on Russia and France and beginning of the First World War
4 August 1914	SPD parliamentary faction approval of war credits and beginning of the "*Burgfrieden*" policy
11 November 1916	Ebert's election as one of three leaders of the party executive of the SPD parliamentary group

14 February 1917	Death of Ebert's son Heinrich in a Macedonian military hospital
6–8 April 1917	Foundation of the Independent Social Democratic Party of Germany (USPD)
5 May 1917	Death of Ebert's son Georg at the Western Front in France
4–13 June 1917	Negotiations of a delegation of Social Democrats under Ebert's leadership in order to prepare an international peace conference of Socialists in Stockholm
July 1917	Interparty Committee and peace resolution of the Reichstag (19 July)
January 1918	Berlin ammunition workers' strike. Ebert member of the strike committee
3 October 1918	Formation of a Reich government with Prince Max von Baden as chancellor and with Social Democrats' participation for the first time
28 October 1918	Constitutional reforms (parliamentarisation)
9 November 1918	Abdication of Kaiser Wilhelm II. Appointment of Ebert as chancellor. Proclamation of the German Republic by Philipp Scheidemann (SPD)
10 November 1918	Formation of the revolutionary government (Council of the People's Deputies) with three SPD (Friedrich Ebert, Philipp Scheidemann, Otto Landsberg) and three USPD deputies (Hugo Haase, Wilhelm Dittmann, Emil Barth). Agreement between Ebert and General Wilhelm Groener
11 November 1918	Signing of the armistice with the Allies by Matthias Erzberger (Centre Party)
12 November 1918	Proclamation of the revolutionary government's reform programme, including the introduction of eight-hour work day and women's suffrage
16–20 December 1918	Reich Congress of Workers' and Soldiers' Councils in Berlin, deciding for parliamentary democracy and for early elections of a National Assembly
29 December 1918	Withdrawal of USPD from the Council of People's Deputies; entrance of Gustav Noske (SPD) and Rudolf Wissell (SPD) into the government
1 January 1919	Foundation of the Communist Party of Germany (KPD) under the lead of Rosa Luxemburg and Karl Liebknecht

5–12 January 1919	January uprising ("Spartacist Uprising") of the radical left in Berlin
15 January 1919	Murder of Rosa Luxemburg and Karl Liebknecht, leaders of the Communist Party
19 January 1919	Elections of the National Assembly, with the SPD wining 37.9 per cent of votes
6 February 1919	Opening of the National Assembly in Weimar, Thuringia, after which the new republic is named: Weimar Republic
11 February 1919	Election of Friedrich Ebert to Reich president with 277 out of 379 votes cast by the National Assembly. Resignation of his National Assembly mandate (13 February)
13 February 1919	Appointment of Philipp Scheidemann (SPD) to head of government (*Reichsministerpräsident*) and of the so-called "Weimar Coalition" of the SPD, Centre Party and German Democrats (DDP)
23 June 1919	Authorisation of the National Assembly's acceptance of the peace treaty by the new government led by Gustav Bauer (SPD).
28 June 1919	Signing of the peace treaty in Versailles by ministers Hermann Müller (SPD) and Johannes Bell (Centre Party)
31 July 1919	Adoption of a constitution by the National Assembly by a count of 262 to 338 votes cast
11 August 1919	Signing of the new Reich constitution by Friedrich Ebert in Schwarzburg (Thuringia)
21 August 1920	Swearing in of Ebert as president according to the new constitution in Weimar
10 January 1920	Official enforcement of the Treaty of Versailles
13–18 March 1920	Kapp-Lüttwitz Putsch; general strike of workers
27 March 1920	Appointment of Hermann Müller (SPD) as new chancellor
6 June 1920	Reichstag elections with heavy losses for the SPD. Weimar coalition loses its majority
25 June 1920	Appointment of Constantin Fehrenbach (Centre Party) as chancellor in minority cabinet of bourgeois parties without the SPD
4–7 December 1920	Defection of left-wing Independent Social Democrats to the KPD

10 May 1921	Appointment of Joseph Wirth (Centre Party) as chancellor
26 August 1921	Murder of the former Minister of Finance Matthias Erzberger (Centre Party)
16 April 1922	Conclusion of the Treaty of Rapallo between Germany and Soviet Russia
24 June 1922	Murder of Foreign Minister Walther Rathenau (DDP)
24 September 1922	Reunification of SPD and the remnants of the USPD
24 October 1922	Decision of the Reichstag to extend Ebert's term in office until 30 June 1925 with a vote of 314 to 76
21 November 1922	Appointment of Wilhelm Cuno (independent) as chancellor. Formation of the so-called "Cabinet of personalities"
11 January 1924	Occupation of the Ruhr by French and Belgian troops
13 January 1923	Proclamation of the Reich government's passive resistance policy
13 August 1923	Appointment of Gustav Stresemann (DVP) as chancellor of a grand coalition (DVP, Centre Party, DDP, SPD). Massive hyper-inflation
26 September 1923	Suspension of passive resistance; imposition of state of emergency
9 November 1923	Putsch in Munich by Adolf Hitler
15 November 1923	Introduction of the Rentenmark, end of inflation
30 November 1923	Appointment of Wilhelm Marx (Centre Party) as chancellor
13 March 1924	Dissolution of Reichstag, new elections on 4 May
20 October 1924	Dissolution of Reichstag, new elections on 7 December
9 December 1924	Beginning of Ebert's libel suit in Magdeburg
23 December 1924	Verdict in the Magdeburg Trial
15 January 1925	Appointment of Hans Luther (independent) as chancellor
28 February 1925	Death of Friedrich Ebert in Berlin
5 March 1925	Funeral of Friedrich Ebert in Heidelberg
26 April 1925	Election of Field Marshal Paul von Hindenburg as new Reich president

Sources and Bibliography

Friedrich Ebert's estate has not survived. Some of his documents he destroyed himself; most of the rest burned in an air raid during the Second World War. Only a few documents have survived. The extensive files from his time in office as president are in the Bundesarchiv Berlin.

Printed Sources

Ebert, Friedrich, Schriften, Aufzeichnungen, Reden. With unpublished reminiscences from the estate, 2 vol., Dresden 1926.

Ebert, Friedrich, Kämpfe und Ziele. Mit einem Anhang: Erinnerungen von seinen Freunden, Dresden [1926].

Mühlhausen, Walter (ed. with the cooperation of Bernd Braun), Friedrich Ebert und seine Familie. Persönliche Briefe 1909–1924, Munich 1992.

Selected Bibliography

Besson, Waldemar, Friedrich Ebert. Verdienst und Grenze, Göttingen 1970[2].

Birkenfeld, Wolfgang, Der Rufmord am Reichspräsidenten. Zu Grenzformen des politischen Kampfes gegen die frühe Weimarer Republik 1919–1925, in: Archiv für Sozialgeschichte (1965), 453–500.

Braun, Bernd/Mühlhausen, Walter, Vom Arbeiterführer zum Reichspräsidenten. Friedrich Ebert (1871–1925). Katalog zur ständigen Ausstellung in der Reichspräsident-Friedrich-Ebert-Gedenkstätte, Heidelberg 2012.

Buse, Dieter K., Friedrich Ebert – Sein Weg zum Politiker von nationaler Bedeutung (1915–1918), Heidelberg 1994[2].

Friedrich Ebert und seine Zeit. Ein Gedenkwerk über den ersten Präsidenten der deutschen Republik, Berlin-Charlottenburg (1926).

Friedrich Ebert 1871–1925. With an introduction of Peter-Christian Witt, Bonn 1980[2].

Friedrich Ebert als Reichspräsident (1919–1925). Konferenz der Friedrich-Ebert-Stiftung zum 80. Todestag, edited by the Friedrich-Ebert-Siftung, Berlin 2005.

Grebing, Helga, Friedrich Ebert – Von der Verantwortung für die Demokratie in Deutschland, Heidelberg 1996.

Harmer, Harry, Friedrich Ebert (Makers of the Modern World), London 2008.

Kolb, Eberhard/Schumann, Dirk, Die Weimarer Republik, Munich 2013[8].

Kolb, Eberhard (ed.), Friedrich Ebert als Reichspräsident. Amtsführung und Amtsverständnis, Munich 1997.

König, Rudolf/Soell, Hartmut/Weber, Hermann (eds.), Friedrich Ebert und seine Zeit. Bilanz und Perspektiven der Forschung, Munich 1991².

Kotowski, Georg: Friedrich Ebert. Eine politische Biographie, vol. 1: Der Aufstieg eines deutschen Arbeiterführers 1871 bis 1917, Wiesbaden 1963.

Möller, Horst, Die Weimarer Republik. Eine unvollendete Demokratie, Munich 2006⁸.

Mommsen, Hans, Friedrich Ebert als Reichspräsident, in: id., Arbeiterbewegung und Nationale Frage. Selected articles, Göttingen 1979, 296–317.

Mommsen, Hans, Aufstieg und Untergang der Republik von Weimar. 1918–1933, Berlin 2004².

Mühlhausen, Walter, Friedrich Ebert – Sein Leben, sein Werk, seine Zeit. Volume accompanying the permanent exhibition in the President Friedrich Ebert Memorial, Heidelberg 1999.

Mühlhausen, Walter, Die Republik in Trauer. Der Tod des ersten Reichspräsidenten Friedrich Ebert, Heidelberg 2005.

Mühlhausen, Walter, Friedrich Ebert (1871–1925) in: Reinhold Weber/Ines Mayer (eds.), Politische Köpfe aus Südwestdeutschland, Stuttgart 2005, 94–105.

Mühlhausen, Walter, Friedrich Ebert 1871–1925, in: Wilhelm von Sternburg (ed.), Die deutschen Kanzler. Von Bismarck bis Merkel, Berlin 2006, 186–209.

Mühlhausen, Walter, Friedrich Ebert 1871–1925. Reichspräsident der Weimarer Republik, Bonn 2007².

Mühlhausen, Walter: Der Reichspräsident zwischen Tradition und Moderne. Zur Rolle Friedrich Eberts in der Republik von Weimar, in: Ute Schneider/Lutz Raphael (eds.), Dimensionen der Moderne, Frankfurt a. M. 2008, 331–346.

Mühlhausen, Walter, Im Visier der Fotografen – Reichspräsident Friedrich Ebert im Bild, Heidelberg 2009.

Mühlhausen, Walter (ed.), Erinnern und Gedenken – 20 Jahre Reichspräsident-Friedrich-Ebert-Gedenkstätte, Heidelberg 2009.

Mühlhausen, Walter, Friedrich Ebert in German Political Memory, in: Institutions of Public Memory. The Legacies of German and American Politicians. Edited by Astrid M. Eckert, Washington 2007, 115–126.

Münch, Ronald A., Von Heidelberg nach Berlin. Friedrich Ebert 1871–1905, Munich 1991.

Peukert, Detlev J. K., Die Weimarer Republik. Krisenjahre der klassischen Moderne, Frankfurt a. M. 1987.

Pyta, Wolfram, Die Weimarer Republik, Opladen 2004.

Schönhoven, Klaus, Reformismus und Radikalismus. Gespaltene Arbeiterbewegung im Weimarer Sozialstaat, Munich 1989.

Winkler, Heinrich August, Von der Revolution zur Stabilisierung. Arbeiter und Arbeiterbewegung in der Weimarer Republik 1918 bis 1924, Berlin/Bonn 1984.

Winkler, Heinrich August, Der Schein der Normalität. Arbeiter und Arbeiterbewegung in der Weimarer Republik 1924 bis 1930, Berlin/Bonn 1985.

Winkler, Heinrich August, Weimar 1918–1933. Die Geschichte der ersten deutschen Demokratie, Munich 1994[2].

Wirsching, Andreas, Die Weimarer Republik. Politik und Gesellschaft, Munich 2000.

Witt, Peter-Christian, Friedrich Ebert. Parteiführer – Reichskanzler – Volksbeauftragter – Reichspräsident, Bonn 2008[4].

Picture Sources

Archiv der sozialen Demokratie der Friedrich-Ebert-Stiftung, Bonn/Germany: cover, p. 25, 42, 49, 52, 84, 88.

Bundesarchiv (Federal Archives), Berlin/Germany: p. 60 (Bild Y 1-26970).

Bundesarchiv (Federal Archives), Koblenz/Germany: p. 75 (Bild 102-00633), 81 (Bild 146-1988-079-19), 99 (Bild 102-00488).

International Institute of Social History, Amsterdam/The Netherlands: p. 20.

Library of Congress, Washington, D. C./USA: p. 7.

National Archives, College Park/USA: p. 63.

Staatsbibliothek zu Berlin – Preußischer Staatsbesitz (State Library Berlin – Foundation of Prussian Cultural Heritage), Berlin/Germany: p. 96 (N 260/ Margarete Hauptmann No. 2102).

Stiftung Reichspräsident-Friedrich-Ebert-Gedenkstätte (Reich President Friedrich Ebert Memorial Foundation), Heidelberg/Germany: p. 13, 15, 17, 30, 34, 41, 68, 72, 76, 101, 108 (2), 110, 112, 117, 120.